BIRDING
Cape Cod

On
Cape Publications

Cape Cod, Massachusetts

All illustrations, including front and back cover art, are by Barry W. Van Dusen.
Maps are by Janet Heywood, edited by Blair Nikula with Joe Gallante.
Book design and typesetting by Joe Gallante, Coy's Brook Studio, Harwich, MA.
Design and production supervision by Adam Gamble.

For more information, additional copies and bulk orders please contact:
On Cape Publications, Inc.
P.O. Box 218
Yarmouth Port, MA 02675
Email: BirdingCapeCod@oncapepublications.com
On the web: www.oncapepublications.com
Toll Free: 1-877-662-5859

Printed in the United States of America.

10 9 8 7 6 5 4 3 2 1

Front cover illustration is of a Willet.
Back cover illustrations are of a Piping Plover (top) and a Least Tern (bottom).
Title page illustration is of Whimbrels.

Table of Contents

Acknowledgments

No project of this magnitude, written by committee, could have been brought to fruition without the generous assistance of many people. It would be impossible to list all those who have contributed in ways both great and small, but we would like to thank those whose work was most important to the final product. First, and foremost, is Blair Nikula, without whose pushing, prodding, and rewriting, this book would still be unhatched in the nest of our imaginations. Robert Prescott, director of the Wellfleet Bay Wildlife Sanctuary, attended to the nearly endless and tedious details of production, and patiently bore the brunt of the contributors' frequent frustrations.

Contributors to the first edition included Janet Aylward, Sally Clifton, Richard Comeau, Blair Nikula, Robert Pease, Robert Prescott, Robert Scott, Charlotte Smith, and Peter Trimble. Jim Baird and Richard Forster encouraged the project in its formative stages, and Wayne Petersen reviewed the original manuscript for accuracy and content. Jonnie Fisk, Diane Reynolds, Mike O'Connor, and John Redfern each offered assistance and insight at various stages of the project.

Contributors to this revision included Richard Comeau, Michael Dettrey, Ed Foster, Greg Hirth, Stauffer Miller, Blair Nikula, Robert Prescott, Alison Robb, Diane Silverstein, Peter Trimble, Robert Vander Pyl, and Eleanor Winslow. Ginie Page and Don Scott reviewed portions of the manuscript for accuracy. Anne Prince, Diane Reynolds, Barbara Stanton, Frank Caruso, and Barbara Hollis edited the manuscript. Blair Nikula compiled and incorporated the revisions and Robert Prescott managed the production. Ned Handy offered legal assistance.

Diane Silverstein marshaled production of this revision, with good humor and grace, gently prodding everyone and keeping things on track. Dick Jurkowski offered encouragement and insight throughout the process.

Dedication

This book is dedicated to the memory of Charlotte Smith, for years the heart and soul of the Cape Cod Bird Club. With good humor and patience, she introduced an uncounted number of people to the joy of birding on Cape Cod.

Also...

In memory of Jonnie Fisk, one of this book's benefactors, who passed away before it fledged. Known to biologists and naturalists for her work as a bird bander and tern warden, Jonnie inspired many, encouraged even more, and entertained legions with her books, lectures, and banding demonstrations.

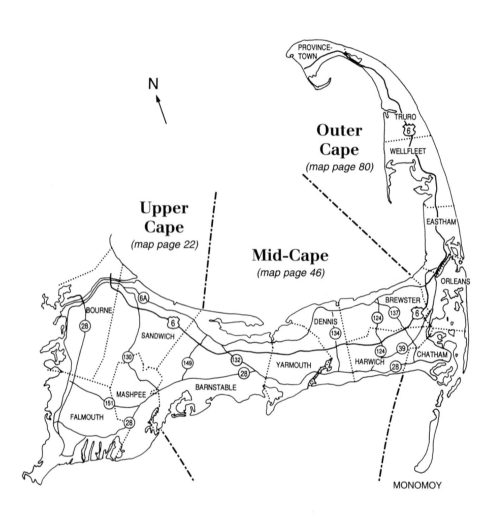

N

Outer
Cape
(map page 80)

Upper
Cape
(map page 22)

Mid-Cape
(map page 46)

PROVINCE-
TOWN

TRURO
6

WELLFLEET

EASTHAM

ORLEANS

BREWSTER

BOURNE

6A

124
137
6

DENNIS

28

SANDWICH

6

134

132

124
39

CHATHAM

YARMOUTH

HARWICH

130

149

28

28

BARNSTABLE

MASHPEE

151

FALMOUTH

28

MONOMOY

Introduction

The "bare and bended arm" of Cape Cod extends eastward for 25 miles from the mainland of Massachusetts, thence northward for another 30 miles to its terminus in Provincetown, and is at no point more than 10 miles wide. The sights and sounds of the sea are never far away. The peninsula is composed of glacial outwash from the final stages of the Pleistocene epoch 10,000 years ago, making it very young in a geological sense.

Fifteen towns are located on Cape Cod, and within many of the towns are smaller villages. The 15 towns constitute Barnstable County, the boundaries of which define the coverage of this guide.

Despite its relative youth, the Cape, as it is known locally and referred to throughout this book, has the oldest recorded ornithological history in North America. As early as 1602, the English explorer Bartholomew Gosnold, who is credited with discovering Cape Cod, wrote of a bird in local waters that came to be known as the Great Auk. Three years later French explorer Samuel de Champlain described what were almost certainly Black Skimmers in the Nauset area. During the 1800s, the peninsula's bird life was studied and observed by such noted naturalists as William Brewster, Edward Howe Forbush, Arthur Cleveland Bent, C.B. Cory, and Henry David Thoreau.

During the first half of the twentieth century, the renowned Ludlow Griscom owned a home in Chatham and spent a great deal of time birding on the Cape with various other luminaries of his time. Also during that period, the Austin Ornithological Research Station was established at what is now the Wellfleet Bay Wildlife Sanctuary. The Cape's popularity among both amateur and professional ornithologists continued, and in 1965 two publications chronicling the area's bird life appeared: *The Birds of Cape Cod* by Norman Hill and *The Birds of the Cape Cod National Seashore* by Wallace Bailey. In 1972, a small group of enthusiasts met and formed the Cape Cod Bird Club, whose membership has since grown to more than 500, making it one of the largest bird clubs in New England. The Cape's ornithological legacy continues unabated.

When to Come

Cape Cod offers the possibility of good birding in any season, though fall traditionally has been the most popular among visiting birders. There is no wrong time to visit for in any season there are an array of species and always the chance for something unusual.

Spring brings a rush of northbound shorebirds, sea ducks, hawks, and songbirds. Historically, spring was considered to be the poorest of seasons in this area, with little to see other than a modest shorebird migration. In *The Birds of Cape Cod,* Hill described the spring migration of land birds as "predictably unimpressive." It is now clear that this characterization was overly disparaging. Increased birding activity in the spring has shown that the Cape hosts an excellent selection of northbound passerines, as well as hawks, and at times the numbers of birds can be impressive.

Though it is true that the magnitude of the migration over the peninsula is far less than over the mainland (as shown by radar studies conducted in North Truro in the late 1960s), the topography of the peninsula, narrowing progressively eastward then northward, results in a concentration of northbound birds as they move "out" the Cape and eventually encounter an expanse of water blocking their flight path. Birders can thus be treated to some fine displays of migrants, particularly from Wellfleet northward, with the largest concentrations typically culminating in Provincetown. Peak numbers of most species occur, on average, several days behind peaks on the mainland. However, the foliage lags even further behind; thus, most of the migration occurs before the trees are fully leaved, making it easier to see the birds than at inland sites.

Summer, if you can bear the overwhelming human tide, offers a number of interesting nesting species, as well as various nonbreeding visitors and the bulk of the southward shorebird migration. Approximately 130 species nest locally, and, although the overall diversity of upland breeding birds is less than on the mainland, some species are more common and easier to find on the Cape. Several noteworthy coastal species, including Piping Plover, Roseate Tern, and occasionally Black Skimmer, nest on some of the barrier beaches and islands. Pelagic birds, particularly those species such as Wilson's Storm-Petrel and Sooty and Greater shearwaters that nest in the South Atlantic during the boreal winter, are common offshore at this season. Other nonbreeding visitors in this season include some of the southern herons (e.g., Tricolored and Little Blue herons) and southern terns (e.g., Royal and Sandwich terns), though all of these are rather rare. The first of the southbound shorebirds often appear by the end of June, and their migration is in full swing by mid-July. The fall migration of warblers and various other songbirds begins as early as late July with the first Northern Waterthrushes and Yellow Warblers and builds during August.

In fall, a steady stream of songbirds passes through, the numbers varying considerably depending on the weather conditions (though sadly, never approaching the levels of years past). The bulk of the thrushes, vireos, and warblers appear in August, with most of these groups moving through in September. Kinglets, sparrows, blackbirds, and others follow in October. The first Peregrine Falcons, Merlins, and accipiters arrive by early September and are seen regularly into November. This is also the time to look for some of the rare but regular western vagrants, including Western Kingbird, Dickcissel, Clay-colored and Lark sparrows, and Yellow-headed Blackbird.

Although the number of shorebirds present begins to drop early in the fall, the variety reaches its peak in September as a few of the rarer species such as American Golden-Plover, Buff-breasted and Baird's sandpipers, and Wilson's Phalaropes appear. Offshore, the pelagic diversity also peaks as the arctic-nesting species such as jaegers and phalaropes join the ranks of shearwaters and storm-petrels. In October large flights of sea ducks appear, predominately scoters initially, followed by eiders and Long-tailed Ducks in November. Large numbers of gannets also slice down the coast during the late fall, providing one of the area's most impressive and dependable avian spectacles. Birding in this season is always enhanced by the knowledge that almost anything can show up—a fact proven time and again!

Many of the Cape's residents believe winter is the best of seasons, since the beaches are largely vacant, and for a short while a sense of peace prevails (though a doubling of the Cape's year-round population over the past 25 years has made seclusion increasingly elusive). The birder, too, can find much to enjoy, because a variety of northern species, combined with lingering "half-hardies," produces a diverse avian potpourri. The combined totals of the Cape's Christmas Bird Counts routinely exceed 140 species. Wintering ducks settle into their preferred haunts along the coast and on freshwater ponds. Alcids, predominantly Razorbills, may appear in quantity along with a few Iceland Gulls or, more rarely, Glaucous Gulls. Northern "irruptive" species such as Rough-legged Hawk, Snowy Owl, Northern Shrike, and the boreal finches may appear, though their numbers vary unpredictably from year to year. The peninsula's slightly warmer climate and abundance of fruit-bearing shrubs induce a variety of species to linger later than they do on the mainland. By carefully birding the appropriate thickets, it is possible to find catbirds, towhees, robins, Hermit Thrushes, Yellow-breasted Chats, and others.

Habitats

The Cape's habitats all have been heavily impacted both by humans and the marine environment. Early accounts indicate that most of the peninsula was heavily forested upon the Europeans' arrival in the area in the 1600s. However, by the late 1800s the Cape had been largely clear-cut, and few trees remained. During the first half of the 1900s, as agriculture diminished and fires were increasingly suppressed, the woodlands regenerated. Today, most of the undeveloped land remaining is wooded with second-growth forest, and open fields have become scarce and much reduced in size.

In the course of natural habitat succession in this area, open fields and pastures are gradually colonized by shrubs, red cedar, and cherry. In time, pitch pine takes hold and eventually shades out the smaller trees and shrubs. As the pitch pine barrens mature, and when fires are absent, oaks begin to invade, and, as they mature, they shade out the pines. In the final stage, rarely achieved on the Cape in recent times, the oak forest gives way to one in which beech becomes the climax species. Unfortunately, the climax habitat on Cape Cod today is all too often characterized by extensive tracts of asphalt and shopping malls.

Most of the area's woodlands today are in a transitional state between pine and oak, and this is by far the most widespread upland habitat. The openness that characterized the Cape at the turn of the century has largely vanished. Fields and pastures exist only in remnant patches, having either been bulldozed or, lacking fires or periodic mowing to keep them open, succeeded to subsequent vegetational stages. Pitch pine barrens too are very fire dependent and are gradually disappearing. In a few very small, isolated patches, primarily in the upper Cape, near-climax beech woodlands exist.

Among the Cape's freshwater habitats are more than 300 ponds, many of them kettle ponds formed by blocks of ice left behind by the last glacial epoch. These ponds range in size from less than an acre to over 700 acres. Additionally, there are several very small rivers and streams, a few stands of cattail marsh (most of them increasingly colonized by the invasive common reed *Phragmites)*, and a number of small white cedar and/or red maple swamps.

The area's marine environments are characterized by numerous bays, harbors, and estuaries. All of these embayments are bordered, at least in part, by parcels of salt marsh, in some cases comprising only an acre or two, in others, covering vast expanses encompassing many hundreds of acres, such as the Great Marsh in Barnstable. Most of these areas are separated from the open water by barrier spits or islands, also of greatly varying size. The smaller spits are typically sparsely vegetated with beach grass and a few other marine-adapted plants and shrubs. The larger spits, such as Sandy Neck in Barnstable, may contain small patches of woodland in their sheltered dune hollows.

The following are characteristic breeding bird species of the major habitats:

Residential areas

Rock Pigeon
Mourning Dove
Chimney Swift (uncommon)
Eastern Phoebe (uncommon)
Barn Swallow
Carolina Wren
House Wren (uncommon)
American Robin
Gray Catbird
European Starling
Chipping Sparrow
Song Sparrow
Northern Cardinal
Common Grackle
Brown-headed Cowbird
Orchard Oriole (rare)
Baltimore Oriole
House Finch
House Sparrow

Fields, pastures, moors, and edges

Green Heron (uncommon and declining)
Northern Bobwhite (uncommon and declining)
American Woodcock
Black-billed Cuckoo (uncommon)
Willow Flycatcher (uncommon)
Eastern Kingbird
Tree Swallow
Eastern Bluebird
Northern Mockingbird
Brown Thrasher (rare and declining)
Cedar Waxwing
Yellow Warbler
Prairie Warbler
Common Yellowthroat

Field Sparrow
Vesper Sparrow (rare and declining)
Savannah Sparrow
Indigo Bunting (rare)
Red-winged Blackbird
American Goldfinch

All woodlands
Red-tailed Hawk
Great Horned Owl
Downy Woodpecker
Northern Flicker
Blue Jay
Common Crow
Black-capped Chickadee

Pitch pine barrens
Northern Saw-whet Owl (rare)
Whip-poor-will (uncommon and declining)
Red-breasted Nuthatch (uncommon)
Hermit Thrush
Pine Warbler
Prairie Warbler
Eastern Towhee
Chipping Sparrow
Purple Finch (rare and declining)

Mixed pine-oak woodlands
Broad-winged Hawk
Ruffed Grouse
Yellow-billed Cuckoo (uncommon)
Eastern Screech-Owl
Red-bellied Woodpecker (uncommon, but increasing)
Hairy Woodpecker
Eastern Wood-Pewee
Great Crested Flycatcher

Red-eyed Vireo
Tufted Titmouse
White-breasted Nuthatch
Brown Creeper (uncommon)
Wood Thrush (uncommon and declining)
Black-and-white Warbler
Ovenbird
Scarlet Tanager
Baltimore Oriole

Freshwater marshes
Mute Swan
Canada Goose
American Black Duck
Mallard
Virginia Rail (uncommon)
Belted Kingfisher
Marsh Wren (uncommon)
Yellow Warbler
Common Yellowthroat
Swamp Sparrow
Red-winged Blackbird

Salt marshes
Osprey
American Oystercatcher (uncommon)
Willet
Saltmarsh Sharp-tailed Sparrow
Seaside Sparrow (rare)
Red-winged Blackbird

Dunes and beaches
Northern Harrier (rare)
Piping Plover
Laughing Gull (uncommon)
Herring Gull

Great Black-backed Gull
Roseate Tern (uncommon)
Common Tern
Least Tern
Horned Lark
Savannah Sparrow

Protected Habitat on Cape Cod

Although Cape Cod has been one of the fastest growing regions in the country over the past several decades, and much habitat has been lost to development, the news is not all bleak. Thousands of acres have been permanently protected, and vigorous efforts continue to preserve as much as possible of what's left. However, few parcels of any size remain, and the extremely high land values make protecting even small tracts very expensive and difficult.

Fortunately, several very large parcels of land were preserved before the development boom struck. Foremost among these is the Cape Cod National Seashore, which was created in the early 1960s. The Seashore encompasses more than 44,000 acres of land on the outer Cape, from Orleans north to Provincetown, including large portions of Wellfleet, Truro, and Provincetown. Creation of the Seashore has been responsible for preservation of much of the Cape's natural habitats and historical charm and character. Most of the best birding spots on the outer Cape are within the Seashore. One shudders to think what the outer Cape would look like today had the national government—and President John F. Kennedy in particular—not had the foresight to save this national treasure.

In 1944, Monomoy Island, which had been used as a bombing range during World War II, was turned over to the U.S. Fish and Wildlife Service and made into a wildlife refuge. Today, Monomoy's 2,700+ acres (now split by the ocean into two islands) comprise one of the best birding sites in the Northeast (page 88). Recently, the Mashpee National Wildlife Refuge was created in the town of Mashpee. Still in the land-acquisition phase, the refuge will be composed of a patchwork of parcels in the Quashnet and Mashpee river watersheds.

Another extremely large tract of federal land is the Massachusetts Military Reservation (MMR), established in the 1930s, which encompasses about 22,000 acres in the upper Cape towns of Bourne, Sandwich, and Falmouth. Although heavily impacted by military activities (including serious pollution of the groundwater in the area, now subject of a massive, multi-million-dollar clean-up effort), the base has thousands of acres of relatively wild habitat, and the military has recently (albeit reluctantly) taken a more environmentally aware approach to management of the base. Extensive grasslands on the base host several breeding species, such as Upland Sandpiper, Eastern Meadowlark, and Grasshopper Sparrow, that have disappeared from the rest of the Cape and exist in only a few places anywhere else in southern New England. There are also vast areas of scrub pine and oak where Whip-poor-wills, Brown Thrashers, and other declining species still occur in some abundance. Unfortunately for birders, the base is closed to visitors.

The state of Massachusetts is also responsible for protecting large parcels of land on Cape Cod, in the form of state parks or state wildlife management areas. Two of the more notable of these are Nickerson State Park in Brewster (1,955 acres, page 70) and the Crane Wildlife Management Area in Falmouth (1,900 acres, page 35).

The individual towns have also protected, to varying degrees, substantial parcels of land for conservation and/or watershed protection. Among the larger and more significant (in terms of wildlife habitat) of these are the West Barnstable Conservation Area (1,100 acres, page 48) in Barnstable, and the Punkhorn Conservation Area (800 acres, page 70) in Brewster. All Cape towns now have land banks in place. Funded by a surtax on real estate sales, the land banks now play one of the most significant roles in land preservation. Additionally, private land trusts operate in many towns and are playing a key role in protecting what is left of wild Cape Cod.

Climate

Cape Cod enjoys — or suffers, depending upon the season and your point of view — a maritime climate. Temperatures are ameliorated by the surrounding water with the result that summers are cooler and winters milder than the adjacent mainland — temperature extremes are not so extreme here.

Winters typically feature raw, damp, and windy weather, though there are frequent exceptions to this pattern. The relatively warm water surrounding the peninsula keeps air temperatures a few degrees above those on the mainland and often results in the Cape receiving rain while it is snowing inland. Although snowfall on the Cape averages less than on the mainland, major snowstorms do indeed occur. When coastal storms pass far enough to the east, it is quite possible for the Cape to be buried under a foot or more of snow while inland areas receive little or none.

Spring is the cruelest of seasons locally, frequently offering little more than unfulfilled expectations. Indeed, local dogma is that the Cape has only three (and some would argue only two) seasons, and spring is not one of them! The ocean turns from ally to adversary in this season, as the waters are much slower than the land to relinquish the winter's chill, and the persistent onshore breezes keep temperatures as much as 15 to 20 degrees (rarely even more) below those away from the water. Not only is the wind cooler, it is moisture laden and fog becomes frequent as the sharp temperature differential between water and air causes condensation. All too often, mainlanders bask in sunny warmth while Cape Codders shiver in a damp soup! Such weather contrasts occur frequently even within the Cape, because the north side, which is several miles "inland" from the prevailing southerly winds, can experience very pleasant conditions while a chilly fog hangs along the southern shore. Indeed, Chatham suffers the dubious distinction of being one of the fog capitals of the East Coast.

During summer, the cool sea breezes turn friendly again and usually keep the Cape from cooking. Heat waves that bake the mainland in 90-plus degree temperatures seldom push the mercury much above 80 degrees locally, especially close to the shore. Fog remains persistent early in the season but gradually wanes as the surrounding waters finally warm a bit and the temperature differential diminishes.

Falls typically are long and delightful. Water temperatures peak early in the season, and the air turns cool and dry. Migrant birds pass through in great diversity and produce some of the best birding of the year. The locals agree this is the time of the year to be on the Cape. Unfortunately, the secret is out, and the summer human congestion now lingers well into autumn.

Getting Around

From the Cape Cod Canal, three main roads, Routes 6, 6A, and 28, run in a generally eastward direction to Orleans. Route 6 (also called the Mid-Cape Highway) is the major highway, limited-access and double-barreled for much of its length, and runs down the terminal moraine—the "backbone" of the Cape. It is by far the fastest and most direct route to many destinations, natural and otherwise.

Route 6A is a scenic, two-lane road, lined with lovely

old homes, and winds along the north side of the peninsula. Travel along Route 6A can be painfully slow during the tourist season, but it is a lovely drive through most of its length and affords access to many fine birding spots on the Cape Cod Bay shore.

Route 28 runs south from the canal to Falmouth, then east along the south shore of the Cape to Chatham, and finally north to Orleans. Through much of its length, it is a heavily congested, two-lane road, which penetrates some of the most heavily developed commercial sections of Cape Cod. During the tourist season, Route 28 can be almost impassable at times, particularly on rainy days when everyone seems to be drifting from one of the innumerable gift shops to the next, and in the late afternoons and early evenings when everyone leaves the beaches en masse and heads out to dinner. At those times, portions of the road in Falmouth, Hyannis, and Yarmouth can be virtually gridlocked. During the off-season the road becomes more tolerable, and it does provide access to many fine birding locales along the Nantucket Sound shoreline.

Five main roads, Routes 130, 149, 132, 134, and 137, all running on a generally north-south axis, connect Routes 6A, 6, and 28. From Orleans to Provincetown, Route 6 is the only highway. This stretch of the highway, particularly through the town of Eastham, is congested and dangerous—drive it with extreme caution.

A source of much confusion is the local usage of the terms "outer Cape," "lower Cape," "mid-Cape," "upper Cape," and "inner Cape" to describe various regions of the peninsula. Ask any five residents to explain these colloquialisms, and you'll likely get at least five different answers. The terms are widely used but have no clear, universally accepted definitions. "Outer" and "lower" are synonymous and refer to the outermost (i.e., farthest from the mainland) portion of the Cape, generally

Chatham to Provincetown, but occasionally including Brewster and Harwich. The rationale, if any, behind the description "lower" to describe this section of the Cape is unknown, but certainly has no connection with its location on a map. The "mid-Cape" usually refers to the area from Dennis to Barnstable. The "upper" or, less commonly, "inner" Cape encompasses Sandwich, Bourne, Falmouth, Mashpee and, in some cases, Barnstable.

A variety of maps and atlases are available at most any local newsstand, pharmacy, supermarket, or convenience store. Although it is not difficult to get lost on the old, winding side roads, you can take comfort in the fact that it is not possible to travel far without encountering one of the main highways, or the water!

Birding by Bicycle

Cape Cod is blessed with a number of bicycle trails that make it pleasant and safe for birding by bicycle. The Cape Cod Rail Trail, 24.5 miles in length, follows the path of old railroad lines from Dennis to Wellfleet. The paved trail, used by walkers and rollerbladers as well, weaves through wooded areas, alongside kettle ponds, and past fields and marshes. You can access the trail at many areas along its route, where parking is generally available. The trailhead is located in the town of Dennis on Route 134, where there is ample parking. Other good starting points are at Depot Street in Harwich, Underpass Road and Route 137 in Brewster, at North Frontage Road in Orleans (just off the Route 6 rotary on the Eastham town line), and at the Marconi site in Wellfleet.

The Cape Cod National Seashore boasts a few short bike routes including the 1.6-mile Nauset Trail in Eastham, the 2-mile Head of the Meadow Trail in Truro, and the hilly, 5.25-mile Provincelands Trail in Provincetown. The Shining Sea Bikeway in Falmouth, the Cape Cod Canal bike path in Bourne, and Nickerson State Park in Brewster are other cycling locations that offer a variety of habitats for your birding pleasure.

Beach Access

All the beaches described in this book are either town, state, or federally owned and are open to the public. During the peak tourist season, from mid-June through Labor Day, admission/parking fees are charged at most beaches. In many cases, it is possible to purchase weekly or seasonal passes, which, if you are planning an extended stay, can be a worthwhile investment. A few of the town-owned beaches are open only to residents during the summer.

Most beach tollbooths are operated from about 9 A.M. to 5 P.M., and only on good beach days. Consequently, you usually can avoid both the fees and the disruptive hordes of sun-worshipping humanity by planning to visit these areas early in the morning or early in the evening, when the birds are less disturbed and more active. Rainy days also offer a less costly and often more productive birding alternative.

The Tides and the "Ocean"

The tides are a critical component in the lives of many Cape Codders, and birders are no exception. The tides in this area, as elsewhere on the East Coast, are semidiurnal: two cycles per day, each about 12.5 hours in duration, making a total of two high and two low tides every 25 hours (approximately).

Most of the local newspapers publish daily or weekly tide charts, and any marina or sporting goods store can supply an annual chart. Many of the charts use Boston tides as a reference and provide a conversion factor for various local sites. In general, tides along the shores of Cape Cod Bay are about 10 to 15 minutes later than Boston; along the oceanside beaches from Provincetown to Chatham they are about 30 minutes later, and along Nantucket Sound, about 45 minutes to an hour or so later. Additionally, in the larger estuaries, such as Pleasant Bay, Nauset Marsh, and the Sandy Neck marsh, the tide in the upper portions of the estuary can lag as much as a couple of hours behind the mouth of the estuary. Average tidal ranges on the Cape vary from nearly 10 feet in Wellfleet to 2 feet or less in the Falmouth area.

The tides are a concern to birders primarily when they are looking for shorebirds. The best tides depend on the location and whether the birds use the area primarily for feeding or roosting. When the tide is a factor at a site, we have indicated so in the text.

The term "ocean" is bandied about a great deal in casual conversation on Cape Cod (as well as in real estate ads that tout "ocean" views). Cape Cod Bay is a large and rather impressive body of saltwater, as is Nantucket Sound; however, neither one is the ocean. Anyone who has spent much time in a boat on the true ocean knows the difference very well. To see the real ocean, you must be on the eastern shore of the Cape from Provincetown south to Chatham—nowhere else!

Pests

Although there are no poisonous snakes or reptiles, nor any dangerous carnivores (though some insist the recently arrived coyote population presents a grave danger!), Cape Cod does have its share of biting insects and, during the warmer months, you will do well to arm yourself with an appropriate repellent.

Ticks are perhaps the most serious concern. Two species are present on the Cape: the larger, more frequently encountered, and relatively innocuous dog tick

(Dermacentor variabilis), and the tiny, dangerous, and nearly undetectable deer tick *(Ixodes dammini)*. The deer tick is a carrier of Lyme disease, which, if untreated, can result in severe arthritis-like conditions as well as cardiac and neurological symptoms. Deer ticks are the size of a pinhead and very difficult to spot. Prior to walking through grassy areas, tuck your pant legs into your socks, and spray your ankles with repellent. Subsequently, check your pants and socks frequently, and, at the end of the day, give your entire body a thorough search. It appears that a deer tick needs to be attached for at least 24 hours before the spirochete is transmitted. The disease's early symptoms include a red ring or rash around the bite and/or flulike symptoms. If detected and attended to early enough, Lyme disease can be treated effectively with antibiotics, usually with no long-term effects.

Mosquitoes are common and widespread throughout the warmer months (May to September), though rarely reaching the intolerable levels that well-traveled birders have likely experienced elsewhere. Greenhead flies *(Tabanus sp)* can be an aggravating nuisance around the region's salt marshes in midsummer. Fortunately, they have a short season, usually from mid-July through mid-August, and the bite, though painful and often bloody, disappears quickly, usually without aftereffects. The wooden boxes placed on stilts around the upper edges of many local salt marshes during the summer, typically blue or green in color, are traps designed to reduce the numbers of these pests. Deerflies *(Chrysops sp)*, cousins of the greenheads, patrol upland areas and are equally voracious and persistent, though also harmless in the long run.

At dawn and dusk on still, warm summer days, nearly invisible clouds of minuscule "no-see-ums," or biting midges *(Ceratopogonidae sp)* emerge to bedevil anyone out and about in favored habitat during those periods. They too concentrate around salt marshes and have a bite that is way out of proportion to their size but, again, the bite's effects are short-lived. To make matters worse, these tiny terrors seem totally oblivious to most commercial repellents and are extremely skilled at finding the tiniest patch of exposed skin.

Local Organizations

The Cape Cod Bird Club conducts several walks each month and holds meetings on the second Monday night of each month, from September through May. Visitors are always welcome at all club activities; check the local papers for current listings or visit their web site at www.massbird.org/ccbc.

Mass Audubon's Wellfleet Bay Wildlife Sanctuary in South Wellfleet (508-349-2615; www.wellfleetbay.org) and the Cape Cod Museum of Natural History in Brewster (508-896-3867) both conduct guided bird walks on a regular basis, usually for a nominal fee. Contact them for their current schedules, or check the listings in the local papers.

Mass Audubon's Voice of Audubon (888-224-6444) is a tape-recorded message of recent bird sightings throughout Massachusetts, and often includes reports from Cape Cod.

Anyone finding an unusual bird in the area should contact the Wellfleet Bay Wildlife Sanctuary or the Bird Watcher's General Store in Orleans (508-255-6974 or 800-562-1512).

Using This Book

In the site descriptions that follow, we have attempted to reduce the amount of tedious, written road directions by relying heavily upon high-quality maps. In our experience, a clearly drawn map is worth hundreds of words.

Written directions are limited to those situations for which a map cannot adequately convey the information necessary to guide the visitor. If you find an area in which you feel this system has fallen short, please let us know.

We have also tried to highlight important locations in the text and on the maps by bolding their names in the text and placing a star next to them on the maps.

Any publication of this sort, particularly one covering as rapidly a developing area as Cape Cod, is doomed to an early obsolescence. We have attempted to postpone this inevitability to the greatest degree possible by limiting coverage primarily to sites that are publicly owned and thus, we trust, protected into the foreseeable future. Privately owned sites have generally been excluded, except in the few instances that there is reason to believe they will remain in a natural state well into the future and that the owners have been particularly tolerant of visitors.

Nevertheless, changes in the local avifauna and habitats are as inevitable as time and tides. If you find any information that needs changes, you come upon errors in any aspect of this publication, or you have any suggestions to offer, we encourage you to write to the Cape Cod Bird Club, c/o Cape Cod Museum of Natural History, 896 Route 6A, Brewster, MA 02631. Good birding!

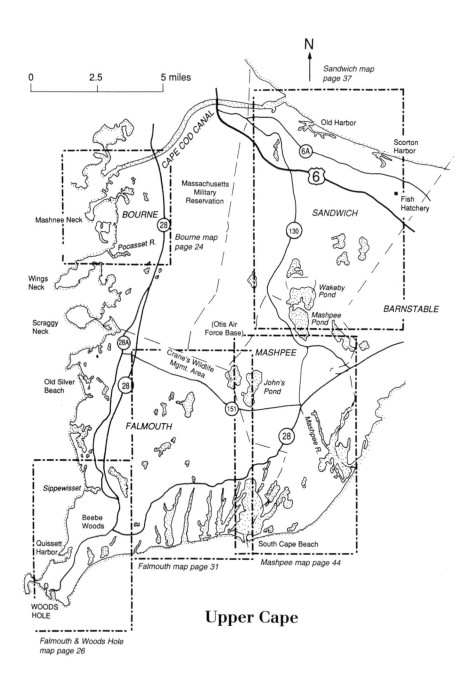

1

The Upper Cape

The area we have defined as the Upper Cape encompasses the towns of Bourne, Sandwich, Falmouth, and Mashpee. Primary attractions for the birder are the extensive shorelines on Cape Cod Bay, Buzzards Bay, and Nantucket Sound, which provide ample opportunities to see migrant and wintering waterfowl; the numerous fresh- and salt-water ponds, particularly in the Falmouth area, that attract large numbers of wintering ducks; and a variety of upland habitats, some of which host a few of the Cape's more unusual breeding passerine species.

BOURNE

The Town of Bourne straddles the Cape Cod Canal. Much of the eastern half of the town lies within the Massachusetts Military Reservation and is off-limits to visitors. Primary birding areas in the town are the Buzzards Bay shoreline, the Bourne (Pocasset) Town Forest, and the Pocasset River system.

The **Buzzards Bay** shoreline, with its many coves and harbors, encompasses many miles, but is mostly privately owned and off-limits to birders. However, there are a few public access points that provide good views of the water. Typical wintering birds in the bay include Common Loon, Horned Grebe, Great Cormorant, Brant,

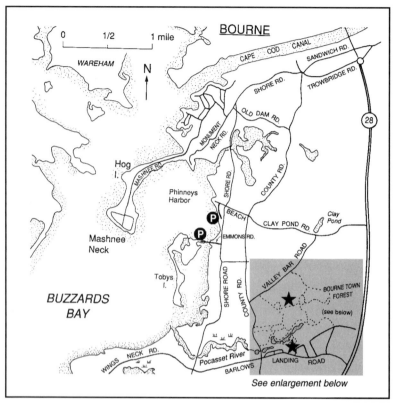

See enlargement below

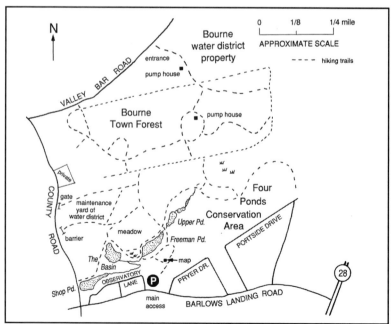

Common Eider, all three scoters, Long-tailed Duck, Bufflehead, Common Goldeneye, and Red-breasted Merganser. One of the largest colonies of Roseate Terns in North America is located a short distance across the bay on Bird Island in Marion, and foraging birds are possible anywhere along the Bourne shoreline during the summer.

Access points include the Monument Beach landing at the end of Monument Avenue, next to the playground (top map page 24); the town marina on Emmons Road (top map page 24), both of which front on Phinneys Harbor; and the town landing at the end of Barlows Landing Road in Pocasset (top map page 24), fronting on Pocasset Harbor. Further south (not shown on the map on page 24) is the town landing and beach on Circuit Avenue on Hen Cove, and the Bourne Conservation Trust property on the west side of Red Brook Harbor. (The trust property on the landward side of the road also has walking trails through mixed woodlands.)

The **Bourne Town Forest** (map page 24) (also referred to as the Pocasset Town Forest on some maps) comprises white pine, pitch pine, and oaks. Black-billed and Yellow-billed cuckoos, Wood Thrushes, Pine and Prairie warblers, Scarlet Tanagers, and rarely an Eastern Bluebird or an Eastern Screech-Owl can be found during the nesting season. Park on Valley Bar Road; dirt roads cross the forest, allowing easy access throughout.

The **Four Ponds Conservation Area** (map page 24) has a series of trails that offer fine birding all year. The ponds are connected by the Pocasset River, and in winter they often have Ring-necked Ducks, Buffleheads, and Hooded Mergansers. White-breasted and Red-breasted nuthatches, Brown Creepers, and Golden-crowned Kinglets are likely along the trails in winter. During the breeding season, Pine Warblers may be found and Prairie Warblers should be listened for in the drier pine woods. Access is available from Barlows Landing Road; watch

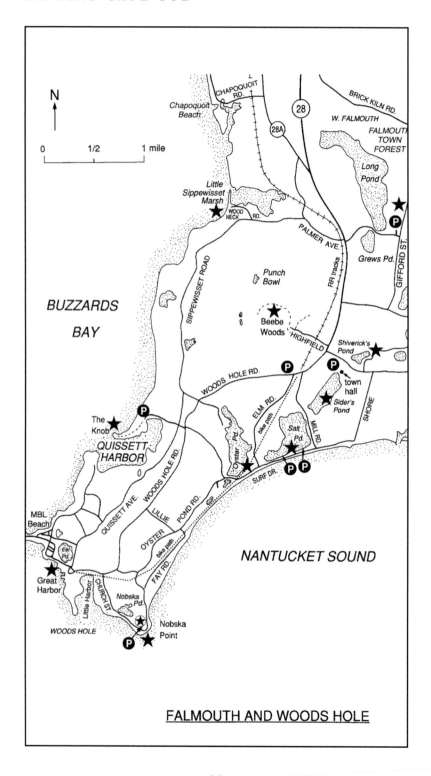

FALMOUTH AND WOODS HOLE

for the small parking area by a sign marking the Four Ponds Conservation Area on the north side of the road.

FALMOUTH

Falmouth is a great spot to bird throughout the year. Of particular interest are the many ponds that harbor a great variety of wintering waterfowl, while lingering fall migrants and semihardy land birds attempt to overwinter in the numerous thickets. Additionally, there are coastal vantage points on Buzzards Bay and Nantucket Sound, estuaries, fields, woods, and a bike path that connects several birding areas from Woods Hole through Nobska Point to Oyster and Salt ponds.

Buzzards Bay can be accessed from several points along the western Falmouth shoreline. Regularly wintering birds include Common Loon, Horned Grebe, Great Cormorant, Brant, Common Eider, all three scoters, Long-tailed Duck, Bufflehead, Common Goldeneye (Barrow's is rare but regular), and Red-breasted Merganser. During the summer both Common and Roseate terns forage along the shoreline. Black Terns are possible from mid-July to mid-September, and Bonaparte's Gulls are regular later in the fall.

Public access to the shore is available at the town landing at the end of Country Road in North Falmouth (not shown on the map on page 26) and at the beach on Quaker Road, where it crosses the Herring River (also not shown on the map on page 26). Further south, there is also access at the beach on Chapoquoit Road (map page 26); The Knob, off Quissett Harbor Road (map page 26); and the MBL (Marine Biological Laboratory) Beach off Gosnold Road in Woods Hole (permit required during the summer) (map page 26).

Little Sippewisset (Wood Neck Road marsh) (map page 26) is a small marsh that hosts a few herons, egrets,

Belted Kingfishers, Saltmarsh Sharp-tailed Sparrows, and occasionally rails. At the end of Wood Neck Road is a view of Buzzards Bay where cormorants, gulls, terns, and wintering sea ducks can be found.

Quissett Harbor (The Knob) (map page 26) has wintering waterfowl, often at close range. Buffleheads, Hooded Mergansers, and Red-breasted Mergansers frequent the harbor, while Horned Grebes, Common Eiders, Long-tailed Ducks, scoters, and Common Goldeneyes feed in Buzzards Bay off The Knob. From the end of The Knob, check for Roseate and Least terns during the summer. The trail out to the point may produce a few migrant or wintering songbirds.

Parking is available near the end of Quissett Harbor Road. From there, walk southwest along the harbor edge and look for the sign indicating "Salt Pond Bird Sanctuary" then follow the trail out the peninsula.

Woods Hole Harbor (Great Harbor) (map page 26) is famous for being home to the Woods Hole Oceanographic Institution, the Marine Biological Laboratory, and the National Marine Fisheries. Woods Hole is an interesting village with some fine restaurants, but it is very congested with limited parking. During the off-season it is usually possible to find a parking spot in town and to walk to the small park bordering the harbor front on Water Street.

Cormorants, sea ducks, occasionally Purple Sandpipers, gulls, and harbor seals are some of the natural attractions. Great Cormorants in winter and Double-crested Cormorants during the warmer months fish the harbor and dry off on the exposed rocks. Common Eiders are the most numerous of the wintering ducks, although a few scoters and rarely a Barrow's Goldeneye or King Eider are present as well. Iceland Gulls are occasional winter visitors and Glaucous, Black-headed, and Little gulls are possible, though rare.

The **Nobska Point** area (map page 26) consists of three sections: Nobska Pond, the lookout at the lighthouse, and the Woods Hole to Oyster Pond bike path. Nobska Pond is surrounded by thickets, which often harbor migrant and wintering land birds. The pond is not very productive, but Mute Swans are usually present and occasionally a few Hooded Mergansers. The lookout at the point offers a wide view of Nantucket Sound, with the Elizabeth Islands to the west and Martha's Vineyard to the south. Cormorants, Common and Red-throated loons, Horned Grebes, Common Eiders, scoters, Red-breasted Mergansers, and gulls may be observed from this prominent bluff. Purple Sandpipers have been spotted on the rocks below. On rare occasions during the late fall, a Little Gull or Black-headed gull has been seen among the more common Bonaparte's Gulls. Both Barrow's Goldeneye and King Eider are possible. The bike path affords good birding along its entire length. Check for land birds during migration and in early winter. As in most of Falmouth, the thickets along this route and the roads that cross it often contain "half-hardy" wintering birds, such as Carolina Wren, Hermit Thrush, Gray Catbird, and Eastern Towhee.

Salt Pond and **Oyster Pond** (map page 26) are accessible from the bike path that passes south of Oyster Pond and along the north side of Salt Pond. To cover the entire path on foot requires considerable time. Birding the specific spots marked on the map where parking is available will give you access to some of the better areas.

The habitat bordering Nantucket Sound consists of thickets, marshes, ponds, small open areas, and deciduous woodlands. Year-round, this region is a worthwhile birding spot and is an enjoyable place to walk or ride. In particular, search the thickets around the ponds and marshes, which often host Carolina Wrens, Cedar Waxwings, sparrows, and other land birds. In early winter, a Yellow-breasted Chat, Orange-crowned Warbler, or some other unusual species will appear on occasion. White-eyed Vireos have nested in this area, and American Woodcocks perform their mating flights along the bike path. Although both ponds are good places to find wintering waterfowl, Salt Pond generally has many more birds and can be checked from Mill Road, Surf Drive, or the bike path. Species frequently present include Great or Double-crested cormorants (depending upon the season), Canvasback, Greater Scaup, Common Goldeneye, Bufflehead, and Hooded Merganser.

Siders Pond and **Shivericks Pond** (map page 26) are both good for ducks during the colder months. Species that may be found here include Pied-billed Grebe, Great and Double-crested cormorants, Canvasback, Greater and Lesser scaup, Ring-necked Duck, Common Goldeneye, Hooded Merganser, and American Coot. Siders Pond, behind the Falmouth Town Hall, is bordered by thickets that can produce migrant and wintering songbirds. Check Siders Pond from the parking lot behind the town hall and Shivericks Pond from Katharine Lee Bates Road in the center of town.

Beebe Woods (map page 26) is a large expanse of deciduous woodlands where forest species such as Wood Thrush, Ovenbird, and Scarlet Tanager nest. House Wrens nest around the summer theater buildings. The thickets and trees around the buildings and at the beginning of the woods trail should be checked for a variety of passerines. The lengthy trail offers a rigorous walk through lovely woods. Park in the conservatory parking lot at the end of Highfield Drive.

The **Falmouth Town Forest** (map page 26) encompasses the Long Pond watershed, Grews Pond, and Goodwill Park. The area is accessible from various points, but the park entrance on Gifford Street (1.1 miles south of Brick Kiln Road or .7 miles north of Jones Road)

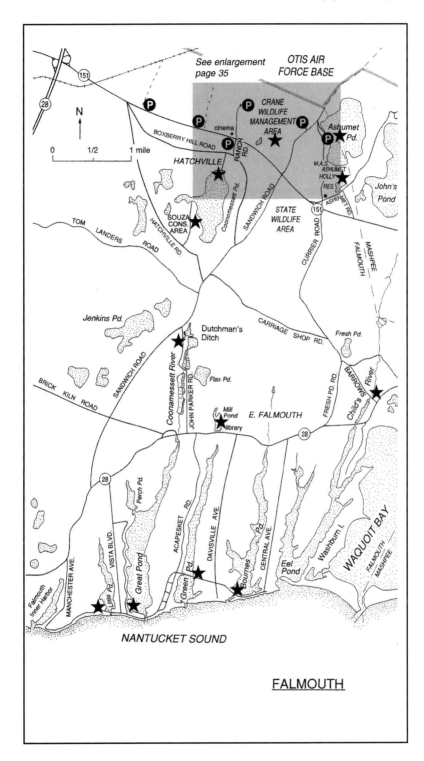

provides the greatest variety of habitats. Park in the lot just off Gifford Street.

Walking west from the parking lot, the first gate on the right provides easy access to the loop road around Long Pond. (Be aware that the first 200 yards of this dirt road is a service entrance for the Department of Public Works and vehicles can materialize very quickly.) The entire loop around Long Pond entails about a 90-minute hike, and there are many trails branching off. Eastern Wood-Pewees, Brown Creepers, Red-eyed Vireos, Ovenbirds, Baltimore Orioles, and Scarlet Tanagers nest here. Spring migrants can be present around Grews Pond, the south and east sides of Long Pond, and near the wet meadow (a 10-minute hike north of the first parking lot). This is also a productive location for flycatchers and swallows. Check both ponds for water-fowl, especially during the winter.

Little Pond, Great Pond, Green Pond, and **Bournes Pond** (map page 31) are among the more productive of the town's brackish coastal ponds and in winter should be checked for Canvasbacks, scaup, Hooded Mergansers, and Bonaparte's Gulls, among the more common species. The edges of these ponds, particularly at their northern edges where streams feed into them, are good birding spots where they are accessible.

Dutchmans Ditch (map page 31) is a small conservation area that contains woodland, marshy edges, a pond, and cranberry bogs. The ponds can be good for wintering Pied-billed Grebe, Mute Swan, Green-winged Teal, Gadwall, American Wigeon, Ring-necked Duck, and American Coot. The woods may have migrant passerines and during winter can have Hermit Thrush, Brown Creeper, Golden-crowned Kinglet, and, rarely, Pine Warbler. The first swallows, blackbirds, and other migrants of the spring often are found here. Access is from John Parker Road, a few hundred yards south of

Sandwich Road; watch for a couple of narrow, rutted dirt roads that lead a short way to the pond.

Mill Pond (map page 31) in East Falmouth usually has an interesting mix of wintering ducks, often including American Wigeon, Gadwall, Ring-necked Duck, Hooded Merganser, and American Coot. Check it from behind the East Falmouth Library off Route 28.

The **Childs River** (map page 31), where it crosses Barrows Road, is another good spot to check in the winter for ducks, particularly Green-winged Teal and Hooded Mergansers, Belted Kingfisher, and a heron or two. Off Route 28 to the south, Whites Landing Road, behind Edwards Boatyard, leads to quiet waters where Hooded Mergansers can be numerous in midwinter.

The **Moonakis River** (map page 44), where it is crossed by Meadow Neck Road, often has a variety of waterfowl, including Mute Swan, Gadwall, scaup, and Hooded Merganser.

Coonamessett Pond (map page 31) is often one of the better spots for wintering waterfowl in Falmouth, including Pied-billed Grebe, Ring-necked Duck, scaup, Hooded and Common Mergansers, Ruddy Duck, and American Coot. The pond can be viewed from town land on the north side of the pond, just west of the country club off Boxberry Hill Road.

American Robin

The **Matthew R. Souza Conservation Area** (map page 31) borders the southwestern corner of Coonamessett Pond and comprises mixed woodland hosting a nice variety of breeding land birds, including Red-breasted Nuthatch, Brown Creeper, Pine Warbler, and Ovenbird. The dirt access road running north from Hatchville Road ends at a cove on Coonamessett Pond where wintering waterfowl are possible.

The **Ashumet Holly Wildlife Sanctuary** (map pages 31, 35), a Mass Audubon property, is an area where several varieties of hollies grow in profusion, and contribute to a pleasant birding experience. The fields may hold migrant sparrows in season, and the thickets and woodlands harbor many of the common land birds

Common Eider

including Carolina Wrens and Pine Warblers. The abundant fruit crop usually attracts flocks of wintering American Robins and Cedar Waxwings as well as a few "half-hardies" such as Gray Catbird and Hermit Thrush. Orchard Orioles may nest here in some years.

The **Crane Wildlife Management Area** (map pages 31, 35), a large tract of over 1,900 acres managed by the Massachusetts Division of Fisheries and Wildlife, has extensive pine barrens and fields, broken by numerous planted hedgerows. This is one of the last places on Cape Cod where nesting Grasshopper Sparrows can be found. Eastern Bluebirds are regular here as well. Prairie Warblers and Field Sparrows are common nesting birds along the field edges, and during migration Northern Harriers, Upland Sandpipers (rare), and Bobolinks might be found in the fields. In the wooded portions of the area, Broad-winged and Red-tailed hawks, Ruffed Grouse, Great Horned Owls, Yellow-billed Cuckoos, Eastern Wood-Pewees, Hermit Thrushes, Pine Warblers, Scarlet Tanagers, and Eastern Towhees nest. Look for Black-billed Cuckoos, Brown Thrashers, and Indigo Buntings along the shrubby, woodland edges. This is one of the few areas left on the Cape where Whip-poor-wills still serenade on summer evenings.

Three parking areas are available on the north side of Route 151: one just to the east of the Nickelodeon Cinema; one just to the west of the cinema; and one at the western

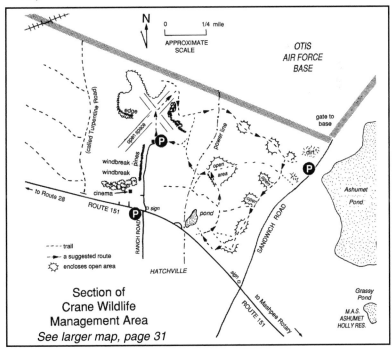

Section of
Crane Wildlife
Management Area
See larger map, page 31

edge of the property at the intersection of Cloverfield Way. Watch for the Massachusetts Division of Fisheries and Wildlife's signs indicating Wildlife Management Areas. Another parking area is located on the west side of Sandwich Road, about .5 miles north of Route 151. Hunting is permitted in season, so Sundays are the only safe days to visit during the fall and early winter. A downloadable map of the area is available at the division's web site: http://www.state.ma.us/dfwele/dfw/.

Ashumet Pond (map pages 31, 35) straddles the Mashpee-Falmouth line but is most easily viewed from the Falmouth side at the town landing off Sandwich Road (on the northwest corner of the pond). During the late fall and winter, waterfowl here often include Pied-billed Grebe, Ring-necked Duck, Common Goldeneye, Hooded and Common mergansers, and American Coot.

Turkey Vulture

SANDWICH

The town of Sandwich has extensive salt marshes, sandy beaches, a few freshwater ponds, cranberry bogs, tracts of deciduous woodland, and a ridge that rises to 200 feet above sea level—one of the highest elevations on Cape Cod. There are also exceptional views of Cape Cod Bay.

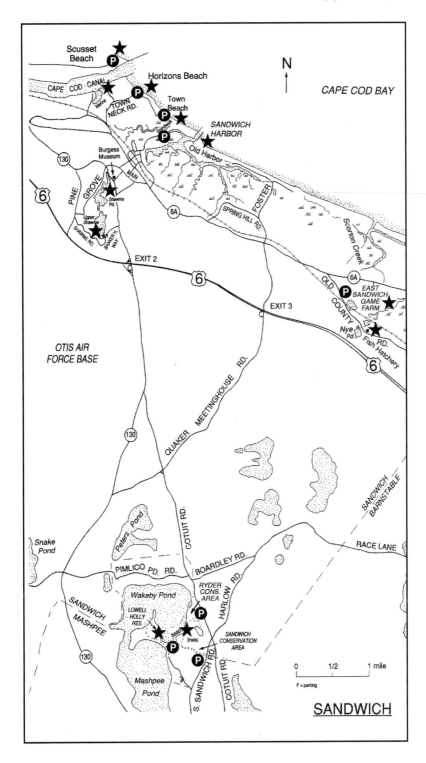

Scusset Beach (map page 37), a state-owned property, lies in the small corner of Sandwich located on the mainland side of the Cape Cod Canal. It is an excellent spot for migrant and wintering waterfowl. The parking lot at the end of Scusset Beach Road provides good access to Cape Cod Bay and the east end of the canal. Common migrant and/or wintering species include Red-throated and Common loons, Horned Grebe, Great Cormorant, Common Eider, all three scoters, Long-tailed Duck, Bufflehead, Common Goldeneye, and Red-breasted Merganser. Harlequin Ducks have been increasingly regular here recently, and this is one of the best spots on the Cape to find King Eider. During the late fall, large numbers of Northern Gannets pass by, and, when winds are strong out of the northeast, a few pelagic species are possible (though the parking lot is too far from the water to permit viewing from the comfort of your car). Check the breakwaters on both sides of the canal for Purple Sandpipers, and the dunes for migrant or wintering Horned Larks, Snow Buntings, Lapland Longspurs, Tree Sparrows, and Savannah Sparrows (including the distinctive "Ipswich" race). The thickets along the road out to the beach may harbor migrant songbirds in the fall, and migrant falcons and accipiters are likely to appear in both spring and fall.

The Sandwich Marina (map page 37), bordering the Cape Cod Canal on Ed Moffitt Drive, is a good place to look for gulls during the winter; Iceland Gulls are regular, while Glaucous and Black-headed gulls are possible. Check the canal for wintering eiders, scoters, and mergansers. During the late fall and winter, especially after storms, there may be a Razorbill, Thick-billed Murre, or Dovekie seeking temporary refuge here.

Horizons Beach (map page 37) (the name refers to the adjacent restaurant), at the end of Town Neck Road, lies on the east end of the Cape Cod Canal, directly across from Scusset Beach (page 38), and has most of the same birds. Large numbers of sea ducks are attracted by the rocky shoreline here, and the beach attracts a few shorebirds, often including wintering Ruddy Turnstones and Purple Sandpipers. A few terns and small gulls are likely in season. Unlike at Scusset Beach, the water can be viewed from the comfort of a car here, making this a better site from which to look for pelagic species during northeasterly storms. A short walk to the west will bring you to the base of the breakwater, from which you can check for birds inside the canal.

Town Neck Beach (map page 37) provides access to both Cape Cod Bay and an extensive salt marsh to the south. It is a good place to see shorebirds in the fall, herons and waterfowl in the spring and fall, nesting Least Terns and Piping Plovers in the summer, and Snow Buntings in the early winter. A boardwalk runs south-west from the end of the parking lot, providing good access to the marsh and the possibility of Saltmarsh Sharp-tailed Sparrow and, if you are very lucky, a Clapper Rail scurrying along one of the tidal creeks. A short walk out the beach east from the parking lot will bring you to the entrance to Old Harbor, where terns and a few shorebirds are possible during the warmer months.

Access is either from the end of Boardwalk Road, which ends in a small parking lot at the south end of the boardwalk, or from Wood Avenue, which ends at the beach and the north end of the boardwalk.

Shawme Pond and **Upper Shawme Pond** (map page 37), in the village center, may have a good assort-ment of wintering waterfowl. Among the masses of pan-handling Ring-billed Gulls, Mallards, and mixed-breed ducks on Shawme Pond you may find Pied-billed Grebes, Mute Swans, a Wood Duck or two, Ring-necked Ducks, Common Goldeneyes, and coots. At Upper Shawme look for Pied-billed Grebes, Gadwalls, American Wigeons, Ring-necked Ducks, and Common Goldeneyes. The beautiful woodlands and thickets surrounding the ponds can provide some excellent land birding in any season. Shawme Pond can be checked from Grove Street along its western shore, and from the Thornton W. Burgess Museum on Route 130. Upper Shawme is accessible from Shaker House Road on the south side of the pond; watch for a small gazebo where there is room to pull off and park.

The **Old Harbor** area (map page 37), across the channel from Town Beach, is worth checking for a variety of shorebirds, terns, and gulls from July to October. In addition to the commoner species, Whimbrel, Willet, Pectoral Sandpiper, Baird's Sandpiper, and Black Tern have been found here. Great Black-backed and Herring gulls and Common and Least terns nest on the point.

Follow Foster Road out to the beach, turn left at the T, park where the soft sand begins, and walk west out the spit. The walk takes about 10 minutes and is very easy. The key to success here is to check the tide charts, looking for the period in the lunar cycle when the high tides are at their lowest (*i.e.*, one of about 9.0 feet or lower in Boston). With a "low" high tide, a shallow puddle surrounded by mudflats is created at the end of the spit, and this puddle becomes a magnet for gulls, terns, shorebirds, and a few other species. The light is best early in the morning so an early high tide will make for very rewarding birding.

The **Fish Hatchery** (map page 37) is a productive birding spot, offering a variety of nesting songbirds including Carolina and House wrens, Wood Thrushes, and, in some years, Orchard Orioles. During the colder months, the thickets may harbor a few "half-hardy" songbirds such as Winter Wren or Hermit Thrush, and the small pond may produce Green-winged Teal,

Wilson's Snipe, and Swamp Sparrow. Nye Pond, which is across the street from the fish hatchery, should be checked for wintering ducks, especially Ring-necked Duck. Park in front of the Sandwich Grange building, on the north side of Old County Road, and walk out back to check the small pond and thickets (there are no maintained trails so a bit of bushwhacking may be necessary).

The **East Sandwich Game Farm** (map page 37) is a 133-acre tract, owned by the state, but managed by the private Thornton Burgess Society in Sandwich. It consists of open fields; spruce, pine, and oak groves; and dense thickets of multiflora rose, bittersweet, and greenbrier bordering salt marsh, tidal flats, and Hoxie Pond. A wooden bridge on the eastern edge of the property connects to Talbot's Point, a town-owned conservation area on the Scorton Creek salt marsh. Nesting species include Osprey, Eastern Phoebe, House Wren, and Carolina wren. During migration, a variety of shorebirds are possible in the salt marsh as well as songbirds in the upland areas. Red-tailed Hawk and Cooper's Hawk are possible at any time, and Sharp-shinned Hawk is frequent from September through May. In winter, this is a good spot to find Green-winged Teal, Killdeer, Wilson's Snipe, and kinglets.

Access is from a small, bumpy, dirt road, running south off Route 6A just west of the Scorton Creek crossing. Bear left at the fork in the dirt road to the small parking area at the water's edge. Trails are present on both sides of the road but are not well marked. A short way south of the parking lot is a small billboard with maps of the area.

The **Sandwich Conservation Area** and the **Lowell Holly Reservation** (map page 37), the latter owned by The Trustees of Reservations, are contiguous properties that front on Wakeby Pond (north) and Mashpee Pond (south). The habitat is mostly woodland, composed of white and pitch pines, oaks, hollies, and maples, but there are also an overgrown cranberry bog, a small pond, and good views of both ponds. Trails through the properties are not always well marked, but it is difficult to get lost.

Birding can be good in any season, but, even if birds are scarce, the area is wonderful to simply wander through. Breeding birds include Ruffed Grouse, Eastern Screech-Owl, Red-bellied Woodpecker, Blue-gray Gnatcatcher, Wood Thrush (increasingly scarce), Northern Parula, Pine Warbler, Ovenbird, American Redstart, and Scarlet Tanager. During migration, a good variety of migrant warblers may be found. Winter birds often include Red-breasted and White-breasted nuthatches, Brown Creeper, Golden-crowned Kinglet, and lingering landbirds such as Gray Catbird and Eastern Towhee. On the lake, look for Common Loon, Pied-billed Grebe, and Common Goldeneye.

There are three entrances to the area. The most popular among birders is located .3 miles north of South Sandwich Road on the west side of Cotuit Road and is known as the Ryder Conservation Area. From the small, dirt, parking area, a trail leads to the overgrown bog, the small pond, and Wakeby Pond. A second entrance to the Sandwich Conservation Area is on South Sandwich Road, .2 miles from Cotuit Road, and winds down to a large dirt parking area near the town beach; a permit is required here in summer, and it is gated during the winter, though you can park at the gate and walk in. This parking area also provides access to both the Lowell Holly Reservation (by walking west along the beach) and to trails leading back to the Ryder Conservation Area. The main entrance to the Lowell Holly Reservation is on the west side of South Sandwich Road, .7 miles from Cotuit Road, where there is space for one or two cars to park and a signboard with a map.

MASHPEE

Located on the south shore of Cape Cod, between the towns of Falmouth and Barnstable, Mashpee has pine barrens, mixed pine-oak woodlands, and a fine barrier beach and estuarine river system. Two prime birding areas containing these habitats are South Cape Beach and the Mashpee River.

Johns Pond (map page 44) frequently has wintering Pied-billed Grebes, scaup, Ring-necked Ducks, Common Goldeneyes, Hooded and Common mergansers, and American Coots. It is best checked from the public beach at the end of Back Road on its northern shore, and from the small gazebo off James Circle on its southern shore.

The **Mashpee River** (map page 44) begins at Mashpee Pond and flows south to Nantucket Sound. Much of the land bordering the river is managed by the Mashpee River Woodlands Committee and The Trustees of Reservations, and encompasses one of the only mature, forested river systems on Cape Cod. During the breeding season, Broad-winged Hawks, Ospreys, Yellow-billed and Black-billed cuckoos, Red-breasted nuthatches, Brown Creepers, Marsh Wrens, Northern Parulas, Pine Warblers, and Swamp Sparrows are among the residents. Winter Wrens, and Golden-crowned and Ruby-crowned kinglets are often present during the fall and early winter. Good birding trails are accessible from the unmarked dirt parking area located on the south side of Route 28 (about 300 yards east of the Mashpee rotary), Quinaquisset Avenue just south of Route 28, Mashpee Neck Road, and River Road. Trail maps and information are posted at some of these locations.

South Cape Beach (map page 44) comprises a barrier beach and salt marsh system on Nantucket Sound, as well as a few small freshwater wetlands and upland pine-oak woodlands. Located at the end of Great Neck

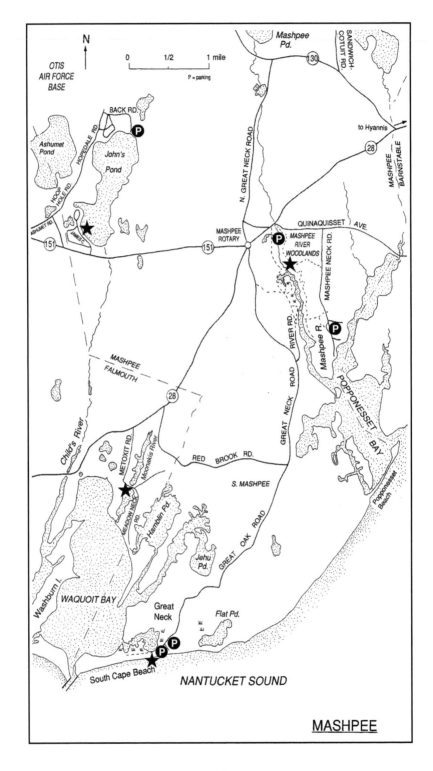

Road, the area is a combination of state- and town-owned lands; there are two parking areas, a state parking area east and a town parking area west (residents only during the summer). Herons, Ospreys, Common, Roseate and Least terns, Horned Larks, and Saltmarsh Sharp-tailed Sparrows may be seen during the warmer months. In the marsh and at the end of the beach, check for shorebirds including nesting Piping Plovers, Spotted Sandpipers, and Willets, as well as a variety of migrant species. Scan Nantucket Sound for loons, Horned Grebes, Northern Gannets, sea ducks, gulls, and terns in season. Along the woodland trails behind the marsh, Ruffed Grouse, Great Horned Owls, Whip-poor-wills, and Pine Warblers are possible. During the late fall and early winter, check the beach for Snow Buntings and the occasional Lapland Longspur, and the breakwater for Purple Sandpiper, which has been seen here on rare occasions.

Washburn Island in Waquoit Bay, visible to the west off the end of the beach, is an interesting but little-known area and can only be reached by boat, kayak, or canoe from the boat landings on Waquoit Bay. Both the island and bay are part of the Waquoit Bay National Estuarine Research Reserve, the headquarters of which are located on the northwestern corner of the bay, off Route 28 in East Falmouth.

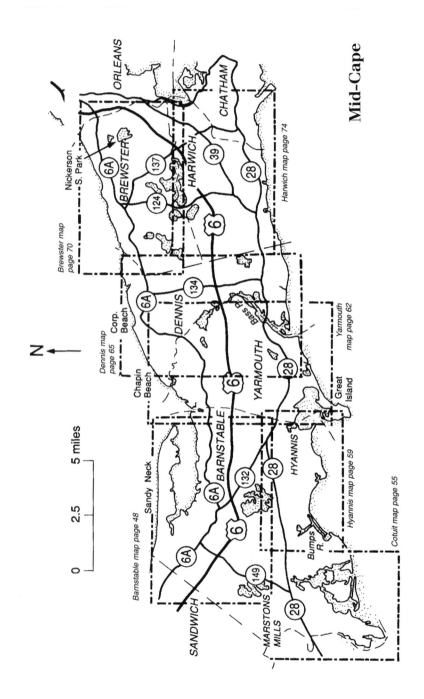

Mid-Cape

ORLEANS

CHATHAM

HARWICH

BREWSTER

Nickerson
S. Park

6A

137

124

39

28

6

Harwich map page 74

Brewster map
page 70

DENNIS

134

6A

Corp.
Beach

Dennis map
page 65

Chapin
Beach

YARMOUTH

6

28

Yarmouth
map page 62

N

BARNSTABLE

Great
Island

HYANNIS

Sandy Neck

6A

132

28

Hyannis map page 59

Bumps
R.

Cotuit map page 55

SANDWICH

6A

6

149

28

MARSTONS
MILLS

Barnstable map page 48

Bass R.

0   2.5   5 miles

2

The Mid-Cape

The Mid-Cape area, as defined here, includes the five towns from Barnstable east to Brewster and Harwich, and offers broad frontage on Cape Cod Bay to the north and Nantucket Sound to the south. It is an area of sharp contrasts, since it contains some of the Cape's most developed and congested sections, such as Hyannis and sections of Route 28 through Yarmouth and Dennis, as well as some of the most wild and beautiful spots. These include such prime birding locations as the magnificent Sandy Neck and Great Marsh system in Barnstable; Chapin Beach, Corporation Beach, and West Dennis Beach in Dennis; the Bells Neck Conservation Area in Harwich; Nickerson State Park in Brewster, and a variety of good waterfowl ponds throughout.

BARNSTABLE

Barnstable is the largest of the Cape's towns, encompassing more than 60 square miles and several villages. There is a sharp contrast between the northern and southern halves of the town. The northern section somehow has remained fairly quiet, with such wild and relatively undisturbed areas as Sandy Neck and the West Barnstable woodlands. The southern portion of town harbors the congested village of Hyannis—the commercial center of Cape Cod—and acre upon acre of densely

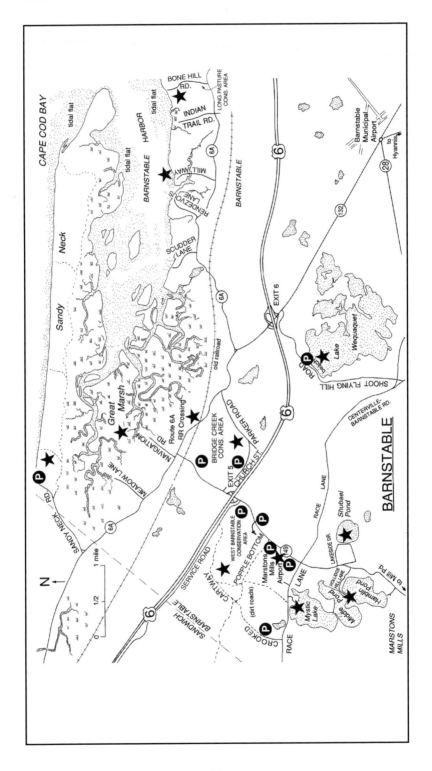

packed residential neighborhoods. However, there is good birding throughout the town, and, should you need to be in Hyannis at some time, do not despair for there is likely to be a productive birding spot somewhere nearby.

Sandy Neck (map page 48) is an expansive barrier beach system, containing a surprising array of upland habitats among the dune hollows. The Sandy Neck parking lot is one of the best places in New England from which to watch pelagics during a northeaster. For best results, the wind must be blowing at least 25 miles per hour from a northeastern direction, and should be the result of a storm that has moved up the coast. Anytime from May to December can be good to see pelagics, although the fall produces them most consistently. From the relative comfort of your car, it is possible to see shearwaters, storm-petrels, phalaropes, kittiwakes, jaegers, and alcids, depending upon the season, as well as rarer species such as Northern Fulmar or Little Gull. (However, be aware that if the wind is blowing very hard, your car may get salt- and sandblasted.)

Rides down Sandy Neck are always an experience but require a four-wheel-drive vehicle and a permit from the town (very expensive for nonresidents). Walking the entire beach takes considerable stamina, because the trek is 6 miles each way, mostly through soft sand. Piping Plovers are common nesters along the outer beach, and one or more small colonies of breeding Least Terns typically are present, most often near the point. Later in the summer, numbers of Common Terns, Roseate Terns, and Laughing Gulls gather here prior to their southward migrations. They are often accompanied by one or more Black Terns, Forster's Terns, or rarer members of their clan. The flats near the point are the best places to look for shorebirds, terns, and gulls at low tide while substantial numbers of these birds may roost on the beach at or near the point during high tide.

Peregrine Falcons and Merlins are regular fall migrants, most likely from late September to mid-October. The pockets of woodland among the dunes, populated with beeches and hollies, may harbor migrant songbirds. Willets nest along the marsh side of the beach. Saltmarsh Sharp-tailed Sparrows nest commonly throughout the marsh and a few Seaside Sparrows usually inhabit the taller grasses along the tidal creeks.

The **Great Marsh** (map page 48), which lies between Sandy Neck and the Barnstable mainland, is one of the largest salt marshes in the state. A variety of herons, shorebirds, raptors, and sparrows are likely in the appropriate seasons. Willets, Saltmarsh Sharp-tailed Sparrows, and Seaside Sparrows all nest, though the latter species is rather scarce. Clapper Rails have been heard with some regularity and may nest, though this has yet to be confirmed. Northern Harriers are common during the nonbreeding season, and migrant or wintering falcons and accipiters are quite likely. This is probably the best place on Cape Cod to find Rough-legged Hawks, though they are not seen every year, and an evening visit may produce a Short-eared Owl or two.

One of the most productive times to bird the area is during "spring" tides (having nothing to do with the season but rather occurring just after the periods of the new and full moons) from late summer through early winter. A tide of 11 feet or more (Boston tide) is best, because these tides will flood much or all of the marsh, forcing a variety of birds into the open, such as herons (often including American Bitterns during the fall), shorebirds, rails (rarely), sparrows, and meadowlarks (late fall). The tide in the upper parts of the marsh runs an hour or two later than in Cape Cod Bay (or Boston), so plan your visits accordingly.

The best access point is the end of Navigation Road (north off Route 6A), which runs right out into the marsh. Park in the small dirt parking area on the right, just before you reach the marsh and walk the rest of the way out. Although it is possible to drive farther out, the road is very rutted and treacherous, and can be covered with water during the highest tides. More than one car has been lost out here!

Another good vantage point for the upper end of the marsh is from a small conservation area at the end of Meadow Lane, which runs north from Route 6A about .9 miles west of Navigation Road. Park at the very small pull-off (room for just one or two cars) on the left at the end of the road and follow the short trail out into the marsh.

The **Route 6A Railroad Crossing** (map page 48) (also known locally as O.K. Hoffmans) in Barnstable has had nesting Willow Flycatchers on the south side of the road for several years. Marsh Wrens linger in the reeds until everything freezes, and Virginia Rails and, more rarely, Soras linger late enough to be recorded on the Christmas Bird Count. Pull off the north side of Route 6A, just west of the railroad tracks and walk back to the section of marsh on the south side of the road (keeping an eye on the traffic along this busy road!).

Barnstable Harbor (map page 48), one of the largest harbors on the Cape, has extensive flats at low tide that often attract a variety of shorebirds and gulls, while waterfowl can be numerous during the colder months. Common and Least Terns are regular during the summer and may be accompanied by one or more Forster's or Black terns during the late summer or fall. Small numbers of shorebirds may be present during migration, and Laughing Gulls are usually numerous during the warmer months, while Bonaparte's Gulls can be common in the late fall. Common Loons, Long-tailed Ducks, Buffleheads, Common Eiders, and Red-breasted Mergansers are among the most numerous of the wintering waterfowl. Careful scoping across the harbor to

Sandy Neck in the distance may reveal a wintering Snowy Owl or Rough-legged Hawk.

Several public access points to the harbor are available, all from the ends of roads running north from Route 6A: Scudder Lane, Rendezvous Lane, Millway, Indian Trail, and Bone Hill Road.

Long Pasture Wildlife Sanctuary (map page 48) is a good spot to hear American Woodcocks on quiet evenings from March through May. From Route 6A, turn north onto Bone Hill Road and proceed a short way to where the road makes a sharp right. Pull into the small parking area on the left, by the Mass Audubon sign. From the parking spot, walk east to the next curve, then go onto the mowed path into the field, and listen carefully. Trails lead north from the parking lot through shrubby upland and past a couple of small ponds where Green Herons and Black-crowned Night-Herons may be found.

The **Bridge Creek Conservation Area** (map page 48) has several areas of interest. The first is along Route 149, at the West Barnstable firehouse. Just behind this building is a small parking area, a kiosk, and a trailhead. This little parking area is a good place in late spring to listen for the buzzy call of the Blue-winged Warbler, a rather rare breeding warbler on the Cape.

Just south of the firehouse along Route 149, take a left onto Church Street and proceed east a short way. This will bring you to another parking area on the left that provides access to this same conservation area. By walking essentially straight north from this parking area, the railroad can be reached. A short walk to the east on the railroad then brings you to the Route 6A railroad crossing (page 51) and its birds. Breeding birds around this parking lot include Red-eyed Vireo, House Wren, Wood Thrush, Black-and-white Warbler, and American Redstart. Between the parking area and the railroad track, Virginia Rail, Ruffed Grouse, Swamp Sparrow, and various warblers have been seen.

The **West Barnstable Conservation Area** (map page 48) offers perhaps the greatest variety of nesting land birds to be found on Cape Cod. A maze of old dirt roads, or cartways, traverse over 1,100 acres of pine-oak woodlands, interspersed with occasional brushy clearings and a broad power-line cut, providing a good opportunity for exploring. Red-tailed Hawks, Ruffed Grouse, Northern Bobwhites, Eastern Screech-Owls, and Great Horned Owls, are present throughout the year; and, during the nesting season, you may find Black-billed and Yellow-billed cuckoos; Eastern Wood-Pewee; Great Crested Flycatcher; Red-breasted and White-breasted nuthatches; Brown Creeper; Wood and Hermit thrushes; Pine, Prairie, Yellow, Black-and-white, and (rarely) Blue-winged warblers; Ovenbird; Scarlet Tanager; Field Sparrow; and Indigo Bunting. In the spring, American Woodcocks perform their courtship displays in the open areas at dusk, and, later in the evening, Whip-poor-wills may be heard, though they have become scarce here. Crooked Cartway, especially the east side, can be good for migrating songbirds on sunny late summer and fall mornings.

This area is accessible from several locations. One of the most popular is from Crooked Cartway, which runs north from Race Lane. The road is gated where it becomes dirt; park at the gate and continue on foot (leaving a trail of crumbs so as not to get lost!). Another access point farther west is from a small dirt parking lot on the north side of Race Lane, just to the east of Drumble Lane. Access is also possible from a small parking area at the beginning of Popple Bottom Road, west of Route 149; a map of the area is available here. Additionally, several dirt roads run south into the area from Service Road (which parallels Route 6), west of Route 149. An adjacent 73-acre conservation property is located to the east, between Route 149 and Osterville-West

Barnstable Road (parking off this road). Maps of these and other town conservation properties are available from the conservation department (200 Main Street, Hyannis, MA 02601); downloadable versions are also available at the town's web site: www.town.barnstable.ma.us/.

The **Marstons Mills Airport** (map page 48), at the intersection of Race Lane and Route 149, is a small, town-owned airfield with grass runways and extensive brushy edges, adjacent to the West Barnstable Conservation Area. During the summer, Northern Bobwhites, Black-billed Cuckoos, Prairie and Yellow warblers, and Field Sparrows are present. Grasshopper Sparrows and Eastern Meadowlarks used to nest but now are seen only rarely. American Woodcocks perform their mating flights in the open areas in the spring while Great Horned Owls hoot from the wooded margins on still evenings. Whip-poor-wills are possible on summer nights. On rare occasions, Rough-legged Hawk and Snowy Owl have been seen here during the winter. You can park at the small dirt parking area on the northeast corner of the airport (along Route 149) or near the inter-section of Route 149 and Race Lane. When exploring the area, stick to the edges and avoid the runways.

The **ponds of Marstons Mills** (map page 55) are good for wintering waterfowl. **Mill Pond,** at the intersection of Route 28 and Route 149, is the smallest but usually most productive pond, particularly for dabbling ducks. Green-winged Teal, American Wigeon (occasionally accompanied by a Eurasian), and Gadwall are regular and may be joined by one or more Pied-billed Grebes, Blue-winged Teal, Northern Pintail, or Wood Ducks. There is often a bit of open water here even when most other ponds have frozen solid. **Hamblin Pond,** off Route 149, usually has a good variety of ducks and rarely the flocks of loafing gulls will contain an Iceland or Glaucous gull. Hollidge Hill Lane (marked private, but

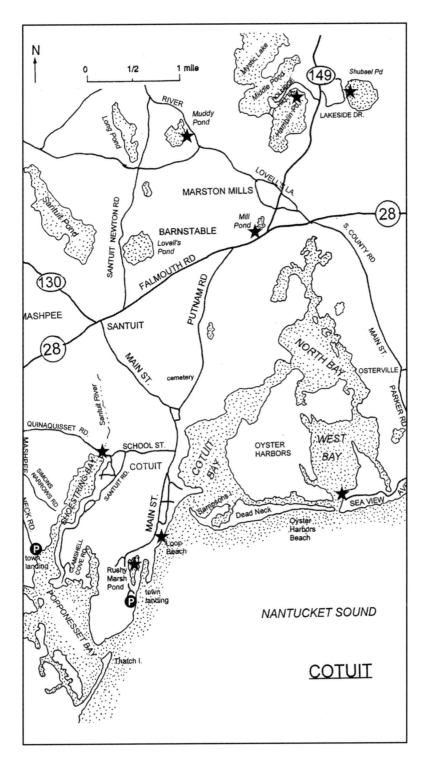

N

0   1/2   1 mile

Mystic Lake

Shubael Pd

149

Middle Pond

LAKESIDE DR.

RIVER

Muddy Pond

Long Pond

Hamblin Pond

LOVELL'S LA.

MARSTON MILLS

28

Santuit Pond

BARNSTABLE

Lovell's Pond

Mill Pond

S. COUNTY RD.

SANTUIT NEWTON RD.

FALMOUTH RD.

130

PUTNAM RD.

MASHPEE

SANTUIT

NORTH BAY

MAIN ST.

OSTERVILLE

28

cemetery

PARKER RD.

Santuit River

QUINAQUISSET RD.

SCHOOL ST.

WEST BAY

OYSTER HARBORS

SIMONS NARROWS RD.

SHOESTRING BAY

COTUIT

COTUIT BAY

MASHPEE NECK RD.

SANTUIT RD.

Sampson's I.

SEA VIEW AV.

MAIN ST.

Dead Neck

Oyster Harbors Beach

CLAMSHELL COVE RD.

P

town landing

Loop Beach

Rushy Marsh Pond

town landing

P

POPPONESSET BAY

NANTUCKET SOUND

Thatch I.

COTUIT

birders are tolerated) leads to a cul-de-sac. Just before the cul-de-sac is a good viewing area to the south over Hamblin Pond and to the north over **Middle Pond.** These ponds are worth checking from October till spring for waterfowl and other birds. Likewise, nearby Lakeside Drive, a loop road east of Route 149, provides good viewing of **Shubael Pond. Mystic Lake** should be checked from the town landing off Race Lane for Pied-billed Grebes, scaup, Common Mergansers, and American Coots. **Muddy Pond** can be good for Wood Ducks during the late summer, and, when water levels are low enough, Wilson's Snipe and Pectoral Sandpipers may be seen in the fall on the muddy western pond shore. The pond is on the west side of River Road, just north of Olde Homestead Drive. There is enough room for one or two cars to pull off on the side of River Road.

Lake Wequaquet (map page 48, 59), one of the largest freshwater lakes on Cape Cod, is an excellent place for wintering waterfowl. Look from the public beach on Shootflying Hill Road for Common Loons, Pied-billed Grebes, Great Cormorants, Canvasbacks, Ring-necked Ducks, scaup, Common Goldeneyes, Hooded and Common mergansers, and other ducks. Bonaparte's Gulls can be numerous during the early winter and may be accompanied by a Common Black-headed Gull. This lake is one of the last bodies of fresh-water to freeze during the winter and can be especially productive when the smaller ponds have iced over.

Shoestring Bay (map page 55) lies on the border between Cotuit and Mashpee. During the winter, Buffleheads, Common Goldeneyes, and Red-breasted Mergansers are likely. Hooded Mergansers, Canvas-backs, and an occasional Northern Pintail have been seen as well. Access is available at the head of the bay and at town landings on both sides of the bay. On the Cotuit side, there is a pair of small dirt landings on the west side of Santuit Road (just south of Popponesset Road). The end of Clamshell Cove Road also provides a view of the lower end of the bay as well as Popponesset Bay to the south. On the Mashpee side, Pirates Cove Landing at the end of Mashpee Neck Road provides a good view of the southern end of the bay, while another view can be had from the end of Simons Narrows Road (the trail down to the water is blocked by large boulders, but you can park in front of the boulders and walk to the shore). You can also look straight down the bay from its head at School Street/Quinaquisset Avenue (the name changes at the town boundary). There's a small pull-off on the north side of the road across from the bay (be careful of traffic) and a small dirt lot on the north side of the road just east of the Santuit River bridge. Take a look up the river, which feeds into the bay, since Hooded Mergansers can be present there.

Rushy Marsh Pond (map page 55) usually has a few waterfowl during the late fall and winter, often including Pied-billed Grebe and scaup, less frequently Green-winged Teal and Canvasback. During migration, Virginia Rails and Soras may lurk in the marshy borders of the pond, as well as in the small marsh across the road to the north. Both Least Bittern and Common Moorhen have been recorded here on rare occasions. The pond and marsh are easily checked from several pull-offs on Main Street, the pond being most visible along its western side. Main Street continues past the pond, ending at a small beach that provides a good view of Nantucket Sound where a variety of wintering ducks are likely.

Loop Beach (map page 55), on Ocean View Avenue in Cotuit, offers a view across the entrance of Cotuit Bay to Sampsons Island. Wintering waterfowl are usually numerous here and may include a Barrow's Goldeneye. Check in the channel and walk a hundred yards or so to the right and look out over Nantucket Sound.

Sea View Avenue (map pages 55, 59), at its western terminus, provides a view of the entrance of West Bay across to Dead Neck and can produce a variety of wintering waterfowl, including Common Loons, Horned Grebes, Long-tailed Ducks, Common Goldeneyes, and, rarely, a Barrow's Goldeneye.

Dowses Beach (map page 59) in Osterville provides a good view of Nantucket Sound, where wintering loons, Horned Grebes, Common Goldeneyes, scoters, and eiders are usually present. In summer, from the east end of the parking lot, you can look across to Long Beach, where a few terns may be present.

Just to the west of Dowses Beach, at the intersection of Sea View Avenue and Wianno Avenue, is a small parking lot that provides a more elevated view of Nantucket Sound.

Craigville Beach (map page 59) provides a good vantage point on Nantucket Sound where a variety of wintering waterfowl can be seen. From the west end of the Craigville Beach parking lots, you can walk west out Long Beach where there is usually a pair or two of nesting Piping Plovers and a few terns. Be careful not to disturb the birds when approaching the nesting areas.

Fifth Avenue (map page 59), off Craigville Beach Road, ends at a small dirt parking lot that provides a nice view of Squaw Island and the Hyannisport marshes. During the warmer months, a few herons, Ospreys, shorebirds, and terns may be present while a variety of waterfowl and Northern Harriers are likely from fall through spring.

Sea Street Beach (map page 59), between Hyannis and Hyannisport, is worth a look throughout the year. Parking in the off-season or early morning is available in the Sea Street Beach parking lot. Walk up the small bluff to the east to scan the water for loons, grebes, Brant, eiders, goldeneyes (occasionally including a Barrow's), and Long-tailed Ducks in winter, and in summer for gulls

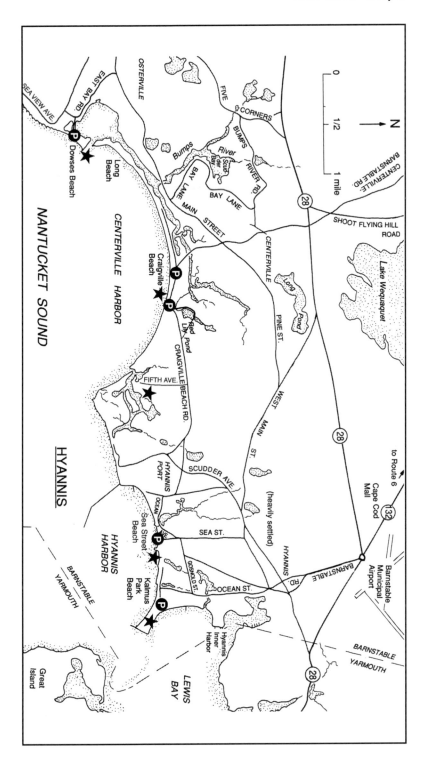

and terns. Walk down the beach to the west to check the area where the creek flows under the road. The tidal marsh on the north side of the road has entertained, in proper seasons, teal, Northern Pintail, Gadwall, Hooded and Red-breasted mergansers, and a few shorebirds.

Kalmus Park Beach (map page 59) is a small barrier beach at the end of Ocean Street in Hyannis and is an interesting place to spend an early-morning hour or two year-round. Least Terns and Piping Plovers are regular nesters, and Horned Larks are likely year-round. In winter you can see a variety of sea ducks, Great Cormorants on the breakwaters, occasionally Snow Buntings, and rarely a Short-eared Owl. The point of land across the channel to the east is Great Island, once the home of C.B. Cory, the turn-of-the-century field ornithologist/naturalist for whom the Cory's Shearwater is named. His home was a gathering spot for collectors, hunters, and naturalists.

Osprey

YARMOUTH

Bounded by Cape Cod Bay to the north and Nantucket Sound to the south, Yarmouth offers a variety of birding habitats, including salt marshes, freshwater ponds, overgrown bogs, and wooded areas.

Hallets Mill Pond (map page 62) usually has a variety of wintering ducks, often including Northern Pintail. During the warmer months, look for herons, shorebirds, and terns. The best birding is about two hours after low tide on the nearby outer beaches, when the mudflats to the east of the bridge at the Keveney Lane-Mill Lane junction are exposed. The pond is easily viewed from Keveney Lane.

Just to the east, off Water Street, a short dirt road leads out to the marshes and the mouth of Barnstable Harbor; this is also a good place to view waterfowl and shorebirds.

Dennis Pond (map page 62) is an area where, with luck, you can encounter migrating warblers and other passerines in May. Do your birding by walking west along the railroad tracks or east on a path parallel to the tracks. You might also walk along Summer Street. Follow the road past the beach to the power lines and check for hawks (Broad-winged Hawks nest in the area) as well as nesting House Wrens, Prairie Warblers, and Field Sparrows along the paths. The trail from Summer Street to Willow Street on the south side of the pond can also be productive for both migrants and residents.

The **Yarmouth Walking Trails Conservation Area** (map page 62) comprises a lovely mix of habitats, extending from Clipper Ship Village on the north side of Route 6A out to Grays Beach. In addition to a variety of common resident woodland and edge species, migrant songbirds are possible in season. The site borders an expansive salt marsh where herons, raptors, shorebirds,

61

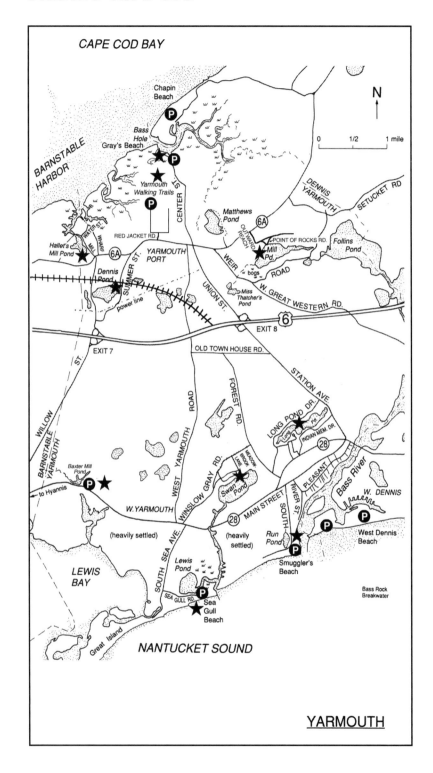

and other marsh species are possible. Access is from a small parking lot located at the west end of Kingsbury Way, just east of the intersection with Belle of the West Road. From the parking lot, the trail crosses a small section of marsh before forking as it enters mixed woodlands. The left-hand trail continues through the woods before ending at the salt marsh where there's a wonderful vista, with Grays Beach to the northeast and the tip of Sandy Neck in the distance to the west. The right-hand trail passes along the edge of the woodland before ending in a residential neighborhood.

Bass Hole (Grays Beach) (map page 62) has a long boardwalk out across the marsh from which you can see herons, shorebirds, and occasionally a rail. At the end, look far west to the sandy dune at the water's edge. This area once hosted a large tern colony, but it has been abandoned in recent years. Nesting Willets and Piping Plovers may also be found, and, if you're lucky, you may see an American Oystercatcher or Black Tern. In fall and winter, the boardwalk affords an excellent vantage point from which to see geese, sea ducks, and gulls. In winter Horned Larks, Snow Buntings, and rarely a Short-eared Owl have been seen around the parking lot.

Mill Pond (map page 62) generally has a variety of wintering waterfowl, which may include Great Cormorant, scaup, Canvasback, or Ruddy Duck among the commoner species. The best place to look from is the end of Point of Rocks Road, off Outward Reach south from Route 6A.

Baxter Mill Pond (map page 62) (simply "Mill Pond" on most maps) abuts, on its eastern shore, a small park on busy Route 28. The pond is worth checking for winter ducks, including Pied-billed Grebe, Gadwall, American Wigeon, and Ring-necked Duck. The adjacent thickets attract a few migrant and nesting land birds.

Sea Gull Beach (map page 62) has several marshy areas on the right as you enter that may have egrets, shorebirds, and rarely a rail. Lewis Pond and the salt marsh on the left host shorebirds and waders; look for Whimbrels during August, especially in the evening. Northern Harriers occur throughout most of the year.

Swan Pond (map page 62) can have wintering Gadwall, Canvasbacks, scaup, Hooded Mergansers and others, which can be seen from a small boardwalk at the end of Meadowbrook Road.

Long Pond (map page 62), in some years, has wintering Canvasbacks, Ring-necked Ducks, scaup, and Hooded Mergansers. The pond can be viewed from vantage points along Indian Memorial Drive, Lakeland Avenue, Ice House Road, and Great Pond Drive.

Bass River (map pages 62, 65) is a good spot to see a few shorebirds and terns in season, as well as wintering loons, cormorants, goldeneyes (including an occasional Barrow's), Buffleheads, Red-breasted Mergansers, and gulls. The parking lot at Smugglers Beach offers good views of the mouth of the river and Nantucket Sound, and you can find other vantage points by the windmill parking lot off River Street and various side roads off Pleasant Street.

DENNIS

Straddling the mid-Cape area is the town of Dennis, which extends from Cape Cod Bay on the north to Nantucket Sound on the south. Dennis has some fine birding spots on both coasts as well as freshwater ponds that attract wintering waterfowl.

Chapin Beach (map page 65) is a lovely barrier beach on Cape Cod Bay, with modest dunes, extensive mudflats, and a sizable salt marsh on its southern edge. At low tide the mudflats attract gulls, terns, and a variety of migrant shorebirds during the warmer months. Nesting Ospreys, Willets, and Saltmarsh Sharp-tailed Sparrows are present in the marsh. From late fall into the

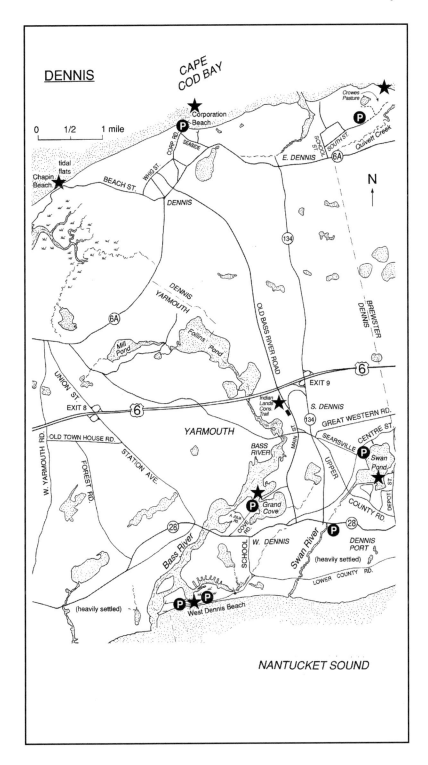

DENNIS

CAPE COD BAY

Corporation Beach

Crowes Pasture

0   1/2   1 mile

tidal flats

Chapin Beach

BEACH ST.

CORP RD.

WHIG ST.

SEASIDE

DENNIS

E. DENNIS

SCHOOL

SOUTH ST.

Quivett Creek

6A

N

134

DENNIS

YARMOUTH

6A

Mill Pond

Follins Pond

OLD BASS RIVER ROAD

BREWSTER

DENNIS

UNION ST.

EXIT 8

6

EXIT 9

U.S. 6

Indian Lands Cons. Trail

S. DENNIS

134

GREAT WESTERN RD.

CENTRE ST.

W. YARMOUTH RD.

OLD TOWN HOUSE RD.

STATION AVE.

FOREST RD.

YARMOUTH

BASS RIVER

SEARSVILLE

Swan Pond

DEPOT ST.

28

Bass River

A.& W. RD.

COVE RD.

Grand Cove

SCHOOL

W. DENNIS

Swan River

UPPER

COUNTY RD.

28

DENNIS PORT

(heavily settled)

LOWER COUNTY RD.

(heavily settled)

West Dennis Beach

NANTUCKET SOUND

65

winter, large numbers of migrant sea ducks pass off-shore, and, when northeasterly winds blow, a variety of pelagic species are possible. In winter, the area often hosts Snow Buntings; rarely a Short-eared Owl, Snowy Owl, or Northern Shrike will reward the fortunate birder.

Corporation Beach (map page 65), 3 miles east of Chapin Beach, can provide excellent birding for loons, grebes, sea ducks, gulls, and alcids in season. Check the flocks of eiders and scoters for King Eider, which occurs here from time to time, and the breakwater for the way-ward Purple Sandpiper. In the fall and early winter, during and immediately following a northeast blow, hundreds of gannets, as well as many other seabirds, may pass by, often at very close range, providing a wonderful opportunity to enjoy these ocean wanderers. This is also one of the most reliable spots on the Cape for Red-necked Grebes; at least a few are usually present, and counts in the early spring have occasionally exceeded 100 birds.

Crowes Pasture (map page 65) (also known as the Quivett Marsh Conservation Area) offers a diversity of habitats including oak and pine woodlands, fields, dunes, beach, and freshwater ponds, as well as a salt marsh and tidal creek. The site attracts a wide range of bird life, including warblers, sparrows, and raptors such as Ospreys, Northern Harriers, Red-tailed Hawks, and Cooper's Hawks. It is hoped that the new grasslands being created here will attract Northern Bobwhites, American Kestrels, Bobolinks, and other grassland birds. Check the field edges for Eastern Bluebirds and Prairie Warblers.

To access the area, turn onto School Street and make a first right onto South Street. Park in the dirt lot across from the cemetery (walk to the marsh to see an active Osprey nesting platform) and then walk the main road and trails leading to the beach. You can also drive past the cemetery down the dirt road about a half-mile to the parking area near the grasslands and bird from there, but this road can be very rutted and muddy and is safely driven only with a high clearance vehicle. Coles Pond is accessed via a grassy road that forks left off the main road.

West Dennis Beach (map page 65), a barrier beach with a variety of habitats, is worth visiting in all seasons. Heading out the long beach parking lot, a salt marsh borders a tidal creek on your right and Nantucket Sound and a ridge of small dunes are on your left. Out in the sound, a distant breakwater is a favorite year-round roost for cormorants and gulls. Piping Plovers, Least Terns, Horned Larks, and Savannah Sparrows nest in the dunes, and a few Common Terns often nest in the sandy areas between the river and the marsh. In the marsh, Willets and Saltmarsh Sharp-tailed Sparrows are common nesters while herons, egrets, and a variety of migrant shore-birds (including Whimbrel) are likely. Horned Larks, "Ipswich" Sparrows, and Snow Buntings are possible throughout the colder months. If you're very lucky, a Short-eared Owl may reveal itself at dusk. The parking lot ends at the Bass River, which in winter is a haven for geese and ducks, including a Barrow's Goldeneye in some years.

Cove Road (map page 65), north from Route 28, offers two good areas for viewing winter waterfowl. At the end of the road is a large parking lot with an excellent view of the Bass River and Grand Cove. Aunt Julia Anns Road, on the right as you return to Route 28, leads to a landing where there is almost always open water in the winter. Buffleheads, Common Goldeneyes (rarely a Barrow's), Red-breasted Mergansers, and others are typically present.

The **Indian Lands Conservation Trail** (map page 65)

provides access to the Cape's longest river, the Bass River, which is tidal and attracts a variety of wintering waterfowl, as well as Belted Kingfishers and Great Blue Herons. The two-mile-long Indian Lands Conservation trail hugs the bank of the river and is good for woodland birds. Access to the trail is at the north end of the Dennis town offices parking lot on Main Street in South Dennis.

Swan Pond and **Swan River** (map page 65) often have a variety of waterfowl, which may include Great Cormorant, Gadwall, Ruddy Duck, and American Coot. There is often open water here when all else has frozen, particularly where the river flows out of the pond (just north of Upper County Road). The pond is appropriately named, because the concentrations of Mute Swans here can be impressive. Good vantage points are available from the river overpass on Upper County Road, from Indian Trail and Clipper Lane off Upper County Road, and from Aunt Laura's Lane off Vester Drive. A small, inconspicuous park, Swan Pond Overlook, on the east side of Center Street (.2 miles north of Whistler Lane), has trails and a view of the pond from its northwestern shore.

BREWSTER

In the mid-Cape area, Brewster extends from Cape Cod Bay south to the town of Harwich. Although population is rapidly increasing in Brewster, numerous conservation areas have been protected, and many productive birdwatching sites should remain available for future generations to enjoy. Prime birding attractions include a number of freshwater ponds, several vantages to Cape Cod Bay, and extensive pine-oak woodlands.

The **Cape Cod Museum of Natural History** (map page 70), located on Route 6A, is a good destination for any naturalist. The museum has a good natural history library with an assortment of bird books. In addition to

Great Horned Owl

the library, the museum has many programs, natural history displays, a gift shop, and outdoor trails. The trails, which are open even when the museum is closed, traverse both upland and wetland habitats, and can provide a variety of avian species in any season. A bird-banding program on Wing Island has captured an impressive variety of migrant and resident songbirds.

The Cape Cod Bird Club holds its evening meetings at the museum on the second Monday of each month from September through June.

Paine's Creek Beach (map page 70) is a good location from which to check Paine's Creek, the adjoining marsh, and Cape Cod Bay. During fall storms, with winds out of the northeast, you may witness a good pelagic show from this vantage point, but you need to be present during high tide or the birds will be too far out to be readily identified. At low tide, the extensive mudflats attract an assortment of migrant shorebirds in season, numbers of Brant during the colder months, and gulls (often including one or

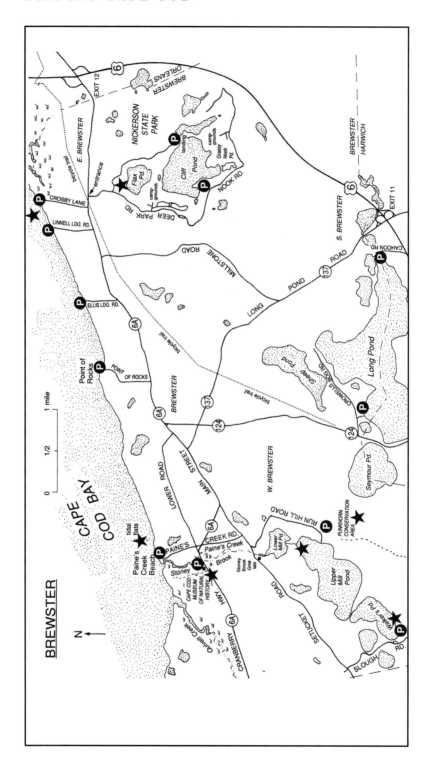

more Lesser Black-backed Gulls) year-round. (Caution: Although you can walk for a mile or so out into the bay during low tide, you must watch carefully for the turning tide in order to make it safely back to shore. Almost every year, someone has to be rescued!) This can be a good place to see migrating and storm-blown waterbirds and seabirds in the fall and early winter, though they are often rather distant (especially at low tide).

Other good vantage points along the Brewster shoreline of Cape Cod Bay, with more or less similar birds as those at Paine's Creek Beach, include the ends of Point of Rocks Road, Ellis Landing Road, and Linnell Road, all of which run north from Route 6A.

Nickerson State Park (map page 70) encompasses more than 1,950 acres. A public campground with over 400 sites operates on a first-come, first-served basis and is usually full during peak summer months. The park includes several clear, freshwater ponds as well as various other small pools and swampy wetlands. The park proper has 7.5 miles of bicycle trails connecting to the Cape Cod Rail Trail, which runs from Dennis to Wellfleet. Birding by bicycle in this area can be a productive and enjoyable experience, providing access to many secluded areas not easily reached otherwise. Cliff Pond is the largest pond in the park and generally the most productive for waterfowl; Common Mergansers can be numerous, and other species may include Pied-billed Grebe, Ring-necked Duck, Common Goldeneye, and Hooded Merganser. The smaller, more secluded ponds often have Green-winged Teal and Wood Ducks during migration (the latter possibly nesting).

Another feature of the park is its consistency in producing owls for those who enjoy listening for the nocturnal calls of these shy residents. Great Horned Owls and Eastern Screech-Owls are relatively common while Northern Saw-whet Owls are less common but heard with some regularity. Late winter to early spring is the most productive time, but you must pick a night with little or no wind for the best results. Nesting species in the park include Cooper's Hawk, Red-tailed Hawk, Hairy Woodpecker, Eastern Wood-Pewee, Great Crested Flycatcher, Red-breasted and White-breasted nuthatches, Brown Creeper, Hermit Thrush, Black-and-white and Pine warblers, Ovenbird, and Scarlet Tanager.

Crosby Landing (map page 70), at the end of Crosby Lane, provides good vantage points of Cape Cod Bay as well as a large salt marsh extending to Namskaket Creek, the border between the towns of Brewster and Orleans. A small trail runs east from the northeastern corner of the parking lot, along the dune/marsh interface, eventually ending at the outer beach. Check the wrack line along the inner beach for Horned Larks year-round, Snow Buntings and Lapland Longspurs from late fall through early winter, and American Pipits during the fall. The marsh may have roosting shorebirds at high tide during migration, occasionally including American Golden-Plover in the fall. Saltmarsh Sharp-tailed Sparrows nest in the marsh, and Ospreys on the platform in the marsh. Northern Harriers are possible from late summer through early spring. You can return to the parking lot via the outer beach where you may see brant, sea ducks, gulls, terns, and possibly pelagic birds (especially if the winds are strong out of the north or east).

Walkers Pond (map page 70) has traditionally been a favorite spot for wintering waterfowl including Pied-billed Grebe, Ring-necked Duck, scaup, Common Merganser, and American Coot. The boat launching area on Slough Road, at the south end of the pond, provides a good vantage point.

Upper Mill Pond (map page 70) is the destination of thousands of Atlantic herring, or alewife, that migrate each spring from the Atlantic Ocean up Paine's Creek to the Stony Brook herring run. The pond is located south of the Stony Brook Mill, which is a popular visitor attraction. Wintering waterfowl often include Pied-billed Grebe, Canvasback, Ring-necked Duck, scaup, Common Goldeneye, and Common and Hooded mergansers. The pond can be checked from a small public landing off Run Hill Road (across from the Brewster water treatment plant), just south of the Punkhorn Parklands parking lot.

The **Punkhorn Conservation Area** (map page 70), a town conservation area, encompasses nearly 800 acres of mixed pine-oak woodland with a few overgrown bogs, and hosts a nice assortment of breeding species typical of that habitat, including Black-billed and Yellow-billed cuckoos, Great Horned Owl, Eastern Wood-Pewee, Great Crested Flycatcher, Red-breasted Nuthatch, Brown Creeper, Hermit Thrush, Pine Warbler, Ovenbird, and Scarlet Tanager. Northern Parulas have been found with some regularity during the summer and may nest. A maze of trails and old dirt roads provide easy (though somewhat confusing) access to the area. Trail maps are available at the small dirt parking lot at the end of Run Hill Road (where the pavement ends). Run Hill Road becomes West Gate Road south of the parking area, and bisects the area, providing easy auto (or bicycle) access for those not wishing to hike the trails. Maps of the area are available from the Brewster Conservation Commission (2198 Main Street, Brewster, MA 02631) and can be downloaded from their web site at: www.town.brewster.ma.us/.

HARWICH

Located in the mid-Cape region, Harwich is bordered to the south by Nantucket Sound and to the north by the town of Brewster. Numerous freshwater ponds, most the result of glacial deposits, are surrounded by mixed oak-pine woodlands. Primary birding attractions include several of the ponds, which host a good variety of wintering diving

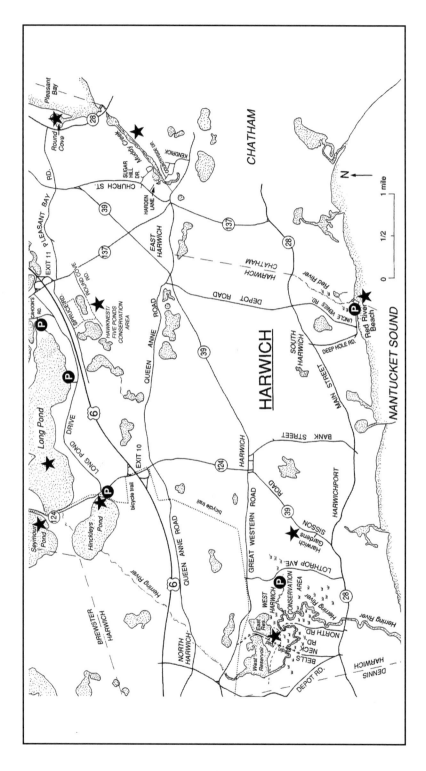

ducks, and the Bells Neck Conservation Area in the south-west corner of town, which encompasses one of the largest expanses of freshwater marsh on Cape Cod.

The **West Harwich Conservation Area** (map page 74) on Bells Neck Road was created to protect the Herring River watershed. A unique area by local standards, this conservation area offers a near wilderness experience in the middle of the hustle and bustle of Cape Cod and encompasses one of the most extensive stands of cattail marsh on the peninsula.

The best place to start birding is between the East and West Reservoirs on Bells Neck Road (south off Great Western Road; park on the side of the road adjacent to the reservoirs). The East Reservoir is shallow and tidal whereas the West Reservoir is deep and fresh, resulting in very different species composition at the two wet-lands. Birding is good during any season, though in summer the vegetation around the East Reservoir grows very thick, making it difficult to get a decent view of the water and flats. During the summer and early fall, scan the mudflats in the middle of the East Reservoir for shorebirds (Killdeer, yellowlegs, Least Sandpiper, and Wilson's Snipe being the most regular), herons, and Least Terns that gather here. During migration this is a good spot for puddle ducks, particularly Green-winged Teal, Gadwall, and American Wigeon. Virginia Rails have nested in the cattails along the edges of the reser-voir and are regularly heard in the fall and early winter.

Check the dead trees in the West Reservoir and along the edges of the water for Ospreys, which often frequent this area, Double-crested Cormorants, and Black-crowned Night-Herons (primarily April to June). Pied-billed Grebes and a few diving ducks may be present here from September through April. During the spring, large numbers of swallows may feed over the reservoir, and Great Horned Owls reside throughout the wooded sections. A walking trail skirts the northern shore of the West Reservoir, from Bells Neck Road to the bicycle trail near the inlet at the northwest corner of the reservoir. This trail provides good views of the water and can be productive for migrant songbirds, particularly on warm spring mornings. Another pleasant and often productive trail runs west from Bells Neck Road along the south side of the West Reservoir, ending at the herring run on the southwest corner of the reservoir.

A bit farther south, Bells Neck Road crosses the Herring River and a large cattail marsh, which can be scanned from the bridge. This is an ideal area to watch and listen for nesting Virginia Rails, Marsh Wrens, and Swamp Sparrows. Northern Parulas have nested along the wooded edges of the marsh. During migration Virginia Rails and Soras are regular, and raptors such as Ospreys, Northern Harriers, accipiters, and Red-tailed Hawks may be seen. From here you can either take the trail easterly through the woods along the north edge of the marsh or retrace your steps back along the road and take a right on North Road. Both will bring you to the North Road footbridge, which offers another lookout over the marsh. The marsh is saltier here, with many fewer cattails. Just before the footbridge an old dirt road runs north along the west edge of the marsh, ending in a small clearing. From there, a narrow, overgrown path leads northeasterly through the common reed and poison ivy to a small wooded island, which provides additional views of the back side of the East Reservoir and marsh, though some bushwhacking may be necessary.

Another access to the northeast corner of this expansive conservation land is the Coy Brook Woodlands parcel, located on the west side of Lothrop Road, just south of the large, blue water tower. From the dirt parking lot, a pleasant trail loops through mixed woodland, occasionally skirting the edges of the cattail marsh and offering another chance for the marsh species listed above.

A popular way to explore the West Reservoir or the Herring River is by canoe or kayak, which can be launched from Bells Neck Road.

The **Harwich Community Gardens** (map page 74), on Route 124/39 (Sisson Road), are on town conservation land that has been set aside for residents to garden. The area is productive in fall for migrant sparrows, and occasionally produces Bobolink, Indigo Bunting, or rarer species such as Clay-colored Sparrow, Blue Grosbeak, or Dickcissel.

Long Pond, Hinckleys Pond, and **Seymour Pond** (map pages 70, 74) feature wintering diving duck popu-lations. Expected waterfowl include Pied-billed Grebes, Canvasbacks, Ring-necked Ducks, scaup, Common Goldeneyes, Common Mergansers, Ruddy Ducks, and American Coots. The three ponds in this area are all accessible from Route 124; it is possible to view most of the ponds from just a few vantage points. Check Hinckleys from the small parking lot across from the Pleasant Lake General Store and Seymour from a small dirt parking lot .9 miles beyond the general store. The eastern portions of Long Pond can be checked from town beaches off Long Pond Drive and Cahoon Road, and the western end from Crowells Bog Road (east from Route 124 just north of the Brewster town line).

Red River Beach (map page 74) is a town-owned barrier beach and a good vantage point for the small Red River Marsh to the north of the parking lot and Nantucket Sound to the south. Red River separates the towns of Harwich and Chatham and provides habitat for a few herons, shorebirds, other marsh birds, and gulls. A variety of sea ducks, terns, and gulls are likely in the sound, depending upon the season. Both King Eider and Barrow's Goldeneye have been seen here.

The **Hawksnest State Park-Five Ponds Conservation Area** (map page 74) is a combination of state and town lands with limited access. This large tract of pine-oak woodland with five ponds is of interest primarily during the breeding season. Most of the typical woodland species are resident here, and it is one of the few places in the state where Northern Parulas nest. None of the ponds are very productive for waterfowl, though from late summer through early fall the shallower ones (e.g., Olivers and Black) often have small groups of Wood Ducks (which may breed in the area), as well as Solitary Sandpiper and a few other shorebirds in dry years.

The best access at present is from Spruce Road, which runs west from Route 137. About .4 miles from Route 137, just past a section of concrete and cable fencing, a narrow, poorly marked trail winds south through the woodlands to the north shore of Olivers Pond. A short distance farther down Spruce Road, a dirt road runs south, passing between Olivers Pond and Hawksnest Pond, before intersecting with Round Cove Road (dirt and unmarked). A right turn on Round Cove Road will take you to a small parking area on Hawksnest Pond, while a left turn will return you to Route 137. Both of these roads can be quite rough and best traversed on foot, mountain bike, or a high-clearance vehicle.

Muddy Creek (map pages 74, 82) on the Harwich/ Chatham border is a small but productive area especially worth checking in the winter when everything else is frozen. Because of numerous springs, portions of the creek tend to stay open even during the coldest spells of winter weather. One of the most productive portions of the creek is located at the end of Harden Lane, off Church Street. In the open water you may find Green-winged Teal and Hooded Mergansers among the more ubiquitous species. Wintering land birds are numerous in the surrounding thickets and at the many feeders in the neighborhood. Additional views of the creek are available from Sugar Hill Drive just to the north of Harden Lane, and from Old Queen Anne Road and Countryside Drive (north off Old Queen Anne Road) on the other side of the creek in Chatham.

Round Cove (map pages 74, 82) is the geographical center of the Cape Cod Christmas Bird Count. This protected cove is worth a quick check during the winter months when Mute Swans, Brant, a few dabbling ducks (rarely including a Eurasian Wigeon), and a lingering heron or shorebird are possible.

Red-winged Blackbird

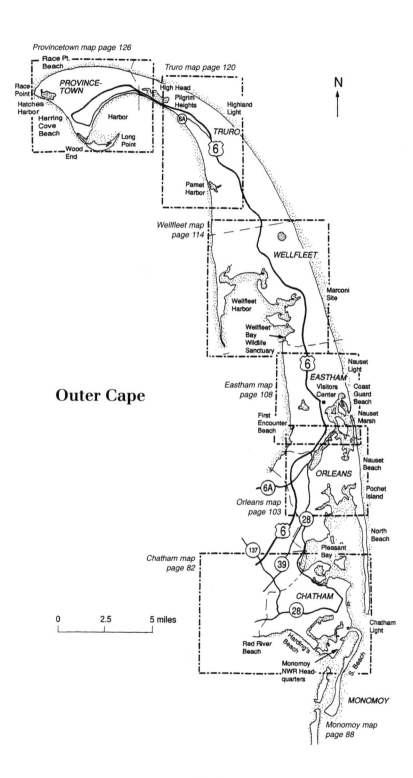

Provincetown map page 126

Provincetown map page 126

Race Pt.
Beach

Truro map page 120

N

Race
Point

PROVINCE-
TOWN

High Head

Pilgrim
Heights

Highland
Light

Hatches
Harbor

Herring
Cove
Beach

Harbor

6A

TRURO

Wood
End

Long
Point

6

Pamet
Harbor

Wellfleet map
page 114

WELLFLEET

Marconi
Site

Wellfleet
Harbor

Wellfleet
Bay
Wildlife
Sanctuary

6

Nauset
Light

Outer Cape

Eastham map
page 108

EASTHAM

Visitors
Center

Coast
Guard
Beach

First
Encounter
Beach

Nauset
Marsh

6A

ORLEANS

Nauset
Beach

Pochet
Island

Orleans map
page 103

28

6

North
Beach

137

Pleasant
Bay

Chatham map
page 82

39

0   2.5   5 miles

CHATHAM

28

Chatham
Light

Red River
Beach

Harding's
Beach

Monomoy
NWR Head-
quarters

S. Beach

MONOMOY

Monomoy map
page 88

3

The Outer Cape

The Outer Cape, from the "elbow" at Chatham to the "clenched fist" of Provincetown, offers some of the top birding sites anywhere in New England. If your time is limited, you would do well to spend most or all of it in this area. Good birding spots abound, but some of the more prominent are: Morris Island in Chatham; Nauset Beach in Orleans; Fort Hill, First Encounter Beach, and Coast Guard Beach in Eastham; the Wellfleet Bay Wildlife Sanctuary in Wellfleet; the Pilgrim Heights area in Truro; and the Beech Forest and Race Point in Provincetown. It is a rare day, indeed, that fails to produce something of interest in one or more of these areas.

CHATHAM

At the "elbow" of Cape Cod, Chatham combines the charm of a rural seaside village with some superb birding possibilities. Chatham presents the visitor with a liquid landscape, since the town is bordered on three sides by water (Nantucket Sound on the south, the Atlantic Ocean on the east, and Pleasant Bay on the north) and is pocketed with numerous bays, inlets, and ponds. The vast expanses of water and extensive shoreline attract large numbers of migrant shorebirds and wintering waterfowl. During the fall migration, particularly when the winds are northwesterly, southbound passerines and

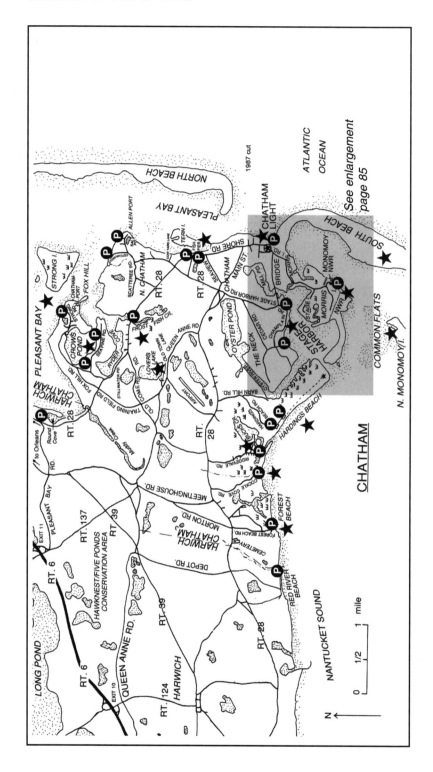

raptors become bottlenecked here. In winter, the numerous thickets and residential plantings provide berries and shelter for a variety of lingering species that are scarce on the colder mainland of Massachusetts during this season. Within the town's borders are two of the premier birding sites in the Northeast: South Beach and the Monomoy National Wildlife Refuge.

Forest Beach (map page 82) is a small barrier beach and salt marsh on Nantucket Sound, worth a quick check in any season. During the warmer months, the salt marsh harbors a few herons, shorebirds (often including Whimbrel during the late summer), and nesting Saltmarsh Sharp-tailed Sparrows. Raptors sometimes use the radio towers as perches, and Ospreys nest on one or more of the large poles in the marsh. Winter brings a variety of sea ducks; Barrow's Goldeneye, King Eider, and Harlequin Duck have been seen here, though all are very rare.

Cockle Cove (map page 82) is another small barrier beach and salt marsh system on Nantucket Sound, and, like Forest Beach, has wintering sea ducks and a few migrant shorebirds and herons.

Bucks Creek (map page 82) is a small, shallow estuary that is of interest primarily in the spring and summer when it attracts herons and shorebirds, particularly yellowlegs, Willets, and American Oystercatchers. It is best when the flats are exposed at low tide, which is approximately three hours after Boston low tide. During higher tides look for herons and roosting shorebirds in the marsh on the south side of the road. For the best vantage, park along the side of the road at the beginning of Ridgevale Road South (just before the end of Ridgevale Road) and walk to the end of the road (a few hundred yards) and out onto the narrow dirt track that runs along the small rise extending into the marsh. The small beach and tidal creek at the end of Ridgevale Road may yield a few shorebirds and terns in season.

Hardings Beach (map page 82) is a lovely 1.2-mile-long barrier beach on Nantucket Sound backed by a narrow expanse of salt marsh. A walk down the beach during the winter may produce a Northern Harrier, Snow Buntings, Horned Larks, "Ipswich" Sparrows, occasionally a Lapland Longspur, and, if you are very lucky, a Short-eared Owl or Snowy Owl. During the warmer months watch in the marsh and at the end of the beach for shorebirds as well as herons, terns, and nesting Saltmarsh Sharp-tailed Sparrows. Piping Plovers and Willets nest here, and American Oystercatchers can often be found on the muddy flats at the entrance to Oyster River. Merlins, Peregrine Falcons, and Sharp-shinned Hawks are possible during fall migration. Access is by foot from the public parking lot (fee during the summer).

Stage Harbor (map page 82, 85), particularly the outer portion, generally has a few wintering ducks and, in late fall, terns and Bonaparte's Gulls, which occasionally are accompanied by a Common Black-headed or Little gull. The best vantage point is from the town landing on Battlefield Road where the light is best in the afternoon. For those willing to hike a bit, other good vantage points are from the end of Hardings Beach (page 85) or the end of the beach on Morris Island.

Morris Island (map pages 82, 85), tucked into the southeast corner of Chatham, offers fine year-round birding. A variety of birds are usually present on this island in any season. Although most of Morris Island and all of adjacent Stage Island are privately owned and generally off-limits to visitors, the federal government owns approximately 56 acres on the east and south sides of Morris Island, part of the Monomoy National Wildlife Refuge (map page 88), and public access is permitted in that portion.

Proceeding out Morris Island Road, check both sides of the causeway for egrets, herons, shorebirds, terns, and small gulls in season. Falcons, accipiters, and Northern Harriers are frequently seen here during migration and winter, and on rare occasions a wintering Short-eared Owl courses over the marsh at dusk. In the fall watch for kingbirds on the wires and sparrows along the roadside and in the shrubs. Small numbers of wintering ducks can be seen in Stage Harbor on the west side of the causeway.

At the end of the causeway, Stage Island Road on the right leads out to Stage Island. Formerly one of the premier land bird "traps" in New England, this small island has suffered heavy residential development, and the resulting loss of habitat and increasingly restricted access has eliminated the birding prospects here—a particularly sad example of what has happened in many portions of Cape Cod. Continuing past Stage Island Road, Morris Island Road leads up onto Morris Island. Do not be intimidated by the "Residents Only" sign. The roads on the island are all private with restricted access, but

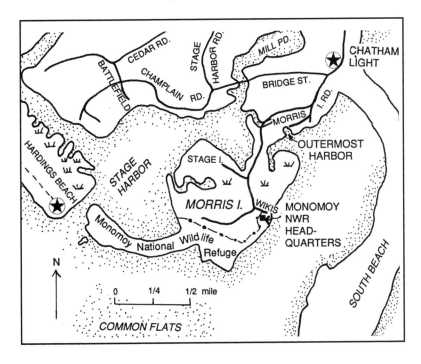

visitors are permitted as far as the first road on the left, Wikis Way, which ends shortly at the Monomoy National Wildlife Refuge headquarters where public parking is available. The parking lot often fills up early in the day during the summer. If the lot is full, return to the causeway, park on the east side of the road, and walk back up the road to the headquarters. A few public exhibits and restrooms are present at the headquarters, and pamphlets, including a bird list, are available.

From the parking lot, a trail leads southeastward to an overlook on the bluff that provides a spectacular view to the east and south. Here, sharp-eyed observers can scope the distant flats on South Beach where it is often possible to pick out the larger, more conspicuous shorebirds, terns, gulls and other waterfowl, rarely a wintering Snowy Owl in the dunes, and occasional seabirds, especially Northern Gannets, over the ocean beyond. During migration watch for hawks and swallows overhead. Belted Kingfishers and Rough-winged Swallows often nest in the cliff face below. Wintering ducks, especially Common Eiders and Long-tailed Ducks, are often numerous in the bay below.

From the overlook, the trail continues south to a set of stairs leading down to the beach below. During the lower half of the tidal cycle, it is possible to continue walking south down the beach to the flats on the south side of Morris Island. Note: This beach is underwater and impassable at high tide. Take careful note of the stage of the tide (usually listed on the bulletin board at the parking lot) before proceeding; if you head down the beach on a rising tide, you may be surprised to find it necessary to wade back to the stairs!

From the south side of Morris Island, Monomoy Island beckons from across the deceptively narrow channel to the south (so near, yet so far!), and South Beach lies to the east. During low tide the mudflats here often attract a variety of shorebirds, which in turn attract migrating Merlins, Peregrine Falcons, Sharp-shinned Hawks, and Northern Harriers. A fall hawk watch conducted from the dunes on the southeast corner of the island since 1998 has documented the passage of hundreds of raptors from late August through November. The flats are favored by American Oystercatchers, Willets, Red Knots, and other shorebirds from spring through early fall. From mid-May to late September, Common and Least terns often fish the channels, and, during the late summer, they may be joined by a few Roseate Terns. Flocks of Double-crested Cormorants routinely pass enroute from roosting sites on Monomoy to feeding areas to the north. During the winter, Common Eiders, Red-breasted Mergansers, Long-tailed Ducks, and other waterfowl are likely.

Continuing west along the beach, watch for Horned Larks in any season and Snow Buntings and an occasional Lapland Longspur in the winter. The beach eventually ends at the mouth of Stage Harbor where you can find a few shorebirds and terns in the summer and fall (best at low tide), and Bonaparte's Gulls (occasionally accompanied by a Little or Common Black-headed gull) during the late fall and early winter. This is also a good spot from which to check for wintering ducks in Stage Harbor.

From the Morris Island parking lot, a second trail runs northeastward a short distance to a wooden platform that provides views northward over salt marsh and tidal bay to the base of South Beach and Chatham Light on the horizon. This is an excellent spot from which to watch for raptors over the marsh and scope the distant flats on South Beach for shorebirds, terns, and gulls.

Monomoy (map pages 82, 88), located off the "elbow" of Cape Cod, is the most northeasterly of a series of islands that fringe New England's southern shoreline.

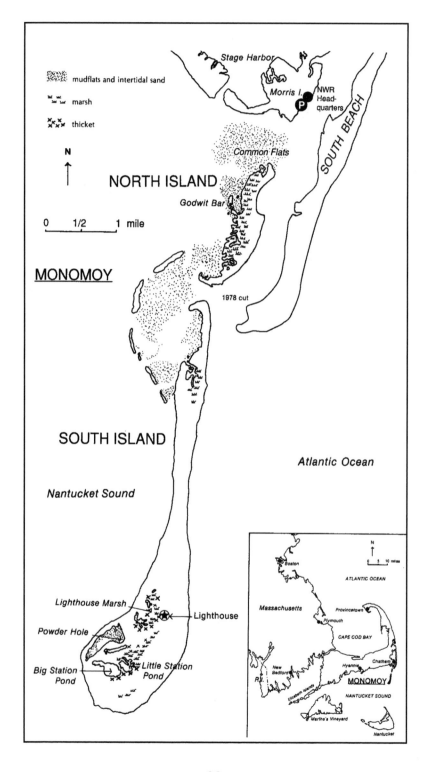

Unlike the other islands, which are glacial formations resulting from the Pleistocene ice sheet, Monomoy is entirely a creation of the sea, composed of sand washed southward from Cape Cod's eroding eastern shore. As such, it is a classic barrier island comprising surf-battered dunes on its eastern shore that gradually flatten out to salt marsh and tidal flats on its western shore. The ocean is continually reshaping Monomoy's approximately 2,700 acres, and at various times in its history, it has been a peninsula, an island, or a series of islands. For the first half of the twentieth century, Monomoy was a peninsula connected to the Chatham mainland at Morris Island and was accessible by beach buggy, which made it a popular birdwatching area, much visited by the famed Ludlow Griscom and other birders of his time. In 1958, an April storm cut through the peninsula just below Morris Island, creating the cut-through that still exists today. Twenty years later, in February 1978, a severe northeaster combined with extremely high tides created a second cut-through about 1.5 miles south of the first cut. Consequently, Monomoy now consists of two islands: a shrinking north island (North Monomoy) approximately 1.5 miles long and a more stable and enlarging south island (South Monomoy) about 6 miles in length.

In 1944 Monomoy became a National Wildlife Refuge, and in 1970 it was afforded even more extensive protection with its designation as a National Wilderness Area.

Birding on Monomoy is considerably different on the two islands. North Monomoy is best visited from May through October when large numbers of shorebirds and gulls are present whereas South Monomoy is best from August through November when migrant landbirds, raptors, waterfowl, and some of the rarer shorebirds can be found.

North Monomoy consists entirely of dunes, salt marsh, and tidal flats and attracts migrating and nesting terns, gulls, and shorebirds. The largest concentrations of birds are generally found one to three hours before or after high tide along the edge of the flats and marsh in a quarter-mile stretch extending from the extreme north end, south to Godwit Bar (see map 88). This area is usually flooded at high tide, forcing the birds farther down the island or over to South Beach to the east.

Formerly one of the largest (in excess of 3,000 pairs) tern colonies in the Northeast was located in the dunes on the extreme north end of the island. The birds were plagued with a variety of problems, however, and now only a handful of Common Terns nest, usually in small, dispersed groups. More recently, a vigorous management program by the U.S. Fish and Wildlife Service has resulted in the development of a huge (10,000+ pairs) colony of Common Terns on the north end of South Monomoy (visible to the south). Roseate Terns can occasionally be found roosting on the flats during the spring and from late July through mid-September. Least Terns have nested sporadically, but their presence is unpredictable. Black Terns are scarce but regular migrants in late spring and again in the early fall, and a few Forster's Terns may be present from late July through the fall. Black Skimmers are occasionally seen in the late summer and have nested in the past.

As many as several hundred pairs of Laughing Gulls once nested among the terns, but they too have moved to South Monomoy. In 1984 a pair of Common Black-headed Gulls nested (unsuccessfully) among the Laughing Gulls, establishing a first breeding record for the United States. Nesting Great Black-backed and Herring gulls have now overrun North Monomoy as well as most of South Monomoy.

Nesting shorebirds are represented by healthy populations of American Oystercatchers and Willets. After an absence of a century or more, both species reestablished themselves as nesters in the early 1970s and are currently thriving with up to a dozen pairs of oystercatchers and many more pairs of Willets occupying the island. A pair or two of Piping Plovers often nest, though they are much more common on the south island, as well as on South Beach to the east.

The prime attraction on North Monomoy is the shorebird migration, which peaks in late May and again in late July through August, during which times several thousand birds may be present. Even more impressive than the numbers is the variety, which is greatest from late August to mid-September. No fewer than 47 species of shorebirds, from every corner of the globe, have been recorded on Monomoy, including such exotics as Eurasian Curlew (second North American record), Wandering Tattler (first East Coast record), Black-tailed and Bar-tailed godwits, Rufous-necked and Little stints, and Long-billed Curlew, along with the somewhat less rare American Avocet, Wilson's Plover, Curlew Sandpiper, and Ruff. The very local Hudsonian Godwit is another shorebird feature, and up to several Marbled Godwits are often present. Occasionally, American Golden-Plover, Wilson's Phalarope, Buff-breasted Sandpiper, or Baird's Sandpiper can be found among the masses of Black-bellied and Semipalmated plovers, Short-billed Dowitchers, Dunlin, Sanderlings, and Semipalmated Sandpipers.

Although waterbirds provide the main attraction on North Monomoy, there are a few other species worth looking for. Horned Larks and Savannah Sparrows nest in the dunes while Saltmarsh Sharp-tailed Sparrows nest commonly throughout the marsh. During migration one should constantly be on the lookout for passing Peregrine Falcons, Merlins, Northern Harriers, and Sharp-shinned Hawks, and occasionally a few land bird migrants can often be flushed from the low shrubs in the dunes. Lapland Longspurs and Snow Buntings are commonly seen from late fall through early winter.

Sand washing through the inlet separating North Monomoy and South Monomoy is deposited just to the west in Nantucket Sound and has created a series of substantial bars, some of which are slowly developing sparse grassy vegetation. Large numbers of Double-crested Cormorants roost on these bars (dubbed by some as "Mini-moy") during the warmer months, and substantial concentrations of shorebirds can be present, either roosting at high tide or feeding on the extensive flats at low tide. Terns also roost here and recently have begun nesting. Unfortunately for birders (but fortunately for the birds!), access to this area is extremely difficult and generally not an option.

South Monomoy is mostly composed of scantily vegetated dunes, and the bird life, with the exception of nesting gulls, Horned Larks, and Savannah Sparrows, is sparse. However, a small portion of the north end of the island is occupied by a very large tern colony during the summer, though this is off-limits to visitors. The primary focus for birders is the bulbous southern terminus of the island, which has freshwater ponds and marshes; dense, wet thickets of bayberry, beach plum, and poison ivy (everywhere!); and a small but productive area of tidal flats. During fall migration, when conditions are right, this area can offer some exciting birding.

The hub of avian activity here is the Station Ponds that lie about a half-mile south and southwest of the lighthouse—Big Station Pond to the west and the smaller, more marshy, Little Station Pond to the east. Numbers of ducks, herons, shorebirds, and gulls frequent these ponds, and the numerous, dense thickets ringing their perimeters attract migrant passerines on good days. Just to the west of the lighthouse is the Lighthouse Marsh, actually a group of very small shallow ponds and wet depressions interspersed among dense thickets and a few scrub pines, some of the very few trees on the island. These ponds are also good places for ducks and herons, and the thickets for migrant land birds; however, much of this area is closed to human traffic to protect nesting and migrant waterfowl. To the north of the lighthouse are extensive beach heather *(Hudsonia sp.)* moors that can be worth checking in the early fall for Buff-breasted and Baird's sandpipers, American Golden-Plover, and Whimbrel. On the southwest corner of the island lies the Powder Hole, an excellent area to see shorebirds, terns, and gulls. Once tidal, sand washing around the southern point has sealed this cove almost completely, choking the flow of water from Nantucket Sound—much the same process that formed Big and Little Station ponds. South and southwest of Big Station Pond are a series of thickets, many of which border small, damp, grassy flats.

On a good fall day on South Monomoy, most of the typical northeast migrants are possible, and day lists exceeding 100 species have been recorded. However, in any coastal migrant land bird trap, the weather is critical to an observer's success, and nowhere is this more evident than on South Monomoy. When the weather is favorable (usually clear skies and light northwest winds) the birding can be very good. Unlike many other coastal traps, there is a distinct lack of landbird habitat here, resulting in a quick exodus of most of the individuals that may be present immediately after the passage of a cold front. Fortunately, the waterbird habitats are more consistently productive, and some good birding is likely on even the slowest of migration days. The Big and Little Station ponds host a remarkable number and variety of waterfowl from late August through November. Daily totals can include more than 20 species of ducks, including Green-winged and Blue-winged teal, Northern

Pintail, Northern Shoveler, Gadwall, American Wigeon, Canvasback, Ring-necked Duck, Greater and Lesser scaup, Hooded Merganser, and Ruddy Duck. One or more Eurasian Wigeons have been found regularly. The shoals offshore attract huge masses of Common Eiders (often numbering into the many tens of thousands) and all three species of scoters. Peregrine Falcons, Merlins, Sharp-shinned Hawks, and Northern Harriers pass through in some numbers during the fall, as do many other diurnal migrants. Short-eared Owls once nested in the dunes but are rarely seen anymore.

The Powder Hole, the west end of Big Station Pond, and the south and east sides of Little Station Pond are generally the best spots for shorebirds, depending upon water levels. In wet years the series of damp "sedge-flats" south of Big Station Pond can be productive. Buff-breasted and Baird's sandpipers are possible in these areas during early fall, as are Wilson's Phalaropes, Stilt and Pectoral sandpipers, and Long-billed Dowitchers.

When planning a visit, be sure to contact the Monomoy National Wildlife Refuge headquarters to obtain current information about restrictions and for information about boating and weather. The address is Monomoy National Wildlife Refuge, Wikis Way, Morris Island, Chatham, MA, 02633 (telephone: 508-945-0594).

Monomoy can be reached only by boat and is not always an easy place to visit. This is particularly true of South Monomoy, which requires almost perfect weather conditions to be accessible. The easiest way to reach North Monomoy is either on a guided tour or with one of the private ferry services. Those visiting for the first time would do well to take one of the guided tours conducted by Mass Audubon's Wellfleet Bay Wildlife Sanctuary. These tours, led by experienced naturalists, are offered to North Monomoy regularly from April through November. Contact the Wellfleet Bay Wildlife Sanctuary

(P.O. Box 236, South Wellfleet, MA 02663; telephone: 508-349-2615; email: wellfleet@massaudubon.org; web site: www.wellfleetbay.org) for its current schedules and rates. For those preferring to explore the islands on their own, one or more private ferry services operate from the Chatham mainland. Contact the refuge headquarters for up-to-date information on these services.

Another means of reaching North Monomoy is by canoe or kayak from the Morris Island causeway. It's a reasonably safe paddle but should be attempted only by experienced paddlers and only when the weather is favorable (i.e., little or no wind and little possibility of fog). When beaching your craft on the island, be certain it is well above the high-tide line and not in a closed area. A floatable, waterproof container for your optics is advisable. Those attempting to take their own craft to Monomoy should be experienced boaters, familiar with the local waters and constantly alert for changes in weather conditions. The weather in the area is very unpredictable and can change suddenly and dramatically. Fog is especially prevalent during the warmer months and can develop literally in a matter of minutes. Treacherous rips are present off the south end of South Monomoy.

Visits to North Monomoy are best during the higher half of the tidal cycle, when the shorebirds and terns are concentrated. The tide has little effect on the bird life of South Monomoy. Keep in mind there are no restroom facilities on either island, and on North Monomoy there is virtually no cover except low scrub or dunes. Attend to personal needs before embarking. Take plenty to drink and some sort of protection from the sun because there is no shade. A lightweight poncho will provide protection from salt spray during the boat trip for both your optics and yourself. Be prepared to wade to and from the boat. Old sneakers are generally the recommended footwear during the warmer months, knee-high rubber boots the remainder of the year. The temperature is generally several degrees cooler than on the mainland, and there is no shelter from the damp wind, so dress accordingly. On South Monomoy, poison ivy is virtually everywhere, growing in loose prostrate carpets throughout the dunes and in head-high bushes in the thickets. It is impossible to bird in the area effectively without some contact with the sinister weed. On occasion, ticks and mosquitoes can be a nuisance. On North Monomoy greenhead flies are on the prowl in July and August. Insect repellents will help, and long pants are recommended for protection against all of these forces—wind, sun, insects, and poison ivy.

When visiting Monomoy, particularly North Monomoy, during the breeding season (May to early August), keep in mind there are birds nesting everywhere the length and breadth of the island. Much of North Monomoy is posted and off-limits during the nesting season, and, no matter where you are, except on portions of the outer beach, you are probably keeping birds off their nests. The best strategy to minimize disturbance is to keep moving and not linger too long in any one place. Visitors should always contact the headquarters ahead of time for information on the current regulations and closures.

South Beach (map pages 82, 88) was once the southern portion of North Beach running south from Orleans. However, in January 1987 a severe winter storm broke through the beach directly east of Chatham Light (page 100), creating a 3-mile-long island. Since then, the north end of the beach has reconnected to the mainland just below Chatham Light and the south end has expanded southward, so the beach is currently about 5 miles long and still growing. Now free of vehicle traffic, South Beach attracts numerous boaters during the summer, but for most of the year it is largely undisturbed and pristine. It has become the premier shorebird site in all of New England, surpassing even its renowned neighbor to the west, Monomoy.

Common Terns

Most of South Beach is composed of dune habitats. However, the flats at the north end of the beach (east of Outermost Harbor), when not overrun with sunbathers, attract small numbers of shorebirds, gulls, and terns in season. The southern third or so of the beach is bordered on the west side by extensive mudflats, and it is this expanding southern portion of the beach that offers the best birding. Large flocks of shorebirds, gulls, and terns roost here at high tide and feed on the expansive flats at low tide. Most of the birds that once roosted on North Monomoy now roost here instead. During the peak of southbound shorebird migration from mid-July through late August, the total number of shorebirds here can exceed 15,000 birds, presenting the observer with an overwhelming spectacle. Numbers during spring migration average about an order of magnitude less.

The most common species, often numbering into the thousands, are Black-bellied Plover, Semipalmated Plover, Red Knot, Sanderling, Semipalmated Sandpiper, Dunlin, and Short-billed Dowitcher. Less abundant, though still often present in the hundreds, are Greater

Yellowlegs, Willet, Ruddy Turnstone, Least Sandpiper, and White-rumped Sandpiper. Hudsonian Godwits often peak at more than 100 birds in early August, making this the best spot on the eastern seaboard to see this scarce shorebird. Uncommon to rare species that can be expected during the late summer and early fall include American Golden-Plover, Marbled Godwit, Western Sandpiper, Pectoral Sandpiper, Buff-breasted Sandpiper, and Long-billed Dowitcher. Careful searching through the masses of shorebirds might also reward the observer with a Curlew Sandpiper or Red-necked Stint, both of which have been found here with some regularity.

Piping Plovers nest commonly, and during August and September groups of 30 to 50 birds can be found tucked into the dunes. Several pairs of American Oystercatchers also nest, and postbreeding flocks in the late summer and early fall may number more than 200 birds. A few Willets now nest as well.

Least Terns frequently nest somewhere on the beach. During the summer and early fall, large flocks of roosting Common Terns, nonbreeders as well as residents from the colonies on Monomoy across the channel, are usually present, especially during the lower half of the tidal cycle. These flocks may contain a few immature Arctic Terns from June through early August, typically nonbreeding first-year birds that have wandered north from their wintering grounds. During the late summer, Roseate Terns, often numbering many hundreds, are present, particularly late in the day. The flocks of loafing gulls often contain one or more Lesser Black-backed Gulls in any season, but especially in the fall.

Northern Harriers regularly course over the dunes in most any season and have nested in some years. During the fall, Peregrine Falcons and Merlins pass through, wreaking havoc among the diminishing flocks of shorebirds. Following the passage of a cold front, a few wayward songbird migrants can often be flushed from the dune grasses. Lapland Longspurs, Snow Buntings, and "Ipswich" Sparrows can be expected during the late fall. This is one of the best areas on the Cape to look for Snowy Owls during flight years.

South Beach also offers good prospects of seeing pelagic birds from land. Shearwaters and storm-petrels are often visible over the ocean to the east during the summer and fall, occasionally close to shore, but are highly unpredictable. Wilson's Storm-Petrels can be abundant offshore during the summer and a few occasionally wander into the channel between the beach and Monomoy. Both Sooty and Greater shearwaters are seen regularly, sometimes by the hundreds. A few Manx Shearwaters appear from time to time, and in some years Cory's Shearwaters can be seen. Parasitic Jaegers are also routinely present from late July through mid-October, at times numbering a dozen or more. They occasionally pass over the flats, panicking the shorebirds and terns, and creating general mayhem. When the weather begins to cool in October, masses of Northern Gannets begin to stream down the coast and by late fall often coalesce into spectacular feeding frenzies just offshore. Black-legged Kittiwakes and Razorbills also become numerous by late fall, lingering into the winter, and can be present by the hundreds or more. More rarely, a few murres or Dovekies may appear at this season.

Although it is possible to walk down South Beach from the vicinity of Chatham Light, it is a very long (exceeding 8 miles round-trip), arduous walk through soft sand and mud, and parking is a problem. At Chatham Light, which is the only access point by foot, parking is limited to 30 minutes, and this limit is vigorously enforced during the warmer months (though generally ignored during the quiet winter months). A much easier means of access during the warmer months is with one of the ferry services that operates from the Morris Island area. At the time of this writing, two such ferries are operating. The Rip Ryder runs from Morris Island (508-945-5450), and Outermost Adventures (508-945-2030) runs from Outermost Harbor just to the north of Morris Island (at the end of Seagull Road). It's a short (10-minute), rather inexpensive (about $10 to $20/person) trip by boat, and the ferries run pretty much on demand, daily (weather permitting) from May through October. Another option, recommended particularly for those unfamiliar with the area, is to take a guided tour with the Wellfleet Bay Wildlife Sanctuary (page 113); there are usually at least one or two trips per week during the prime birding season. The ambitious birder can launch a canoe or kayak from the Morris Island causeway. It's a fairly safe trip if the weather is favorable, but keep an eye on the many powerboats cruising the waters!

Like most barrier beaches fronting the ocean, South Beach is constantly changing, and visiting birders would be wise to check on current conditions before scheduling a trip. Scientists studying the area predict that the northern end of the beach will eventually break through again at some point, while the southern end continues to expand and will eventually connect to South Monomoy. Local birders are watching this geological metamorphosis with great interest, eager to see how the area's abundant avifauna adapts to the changes in this dynamic corner of the world.

Chatham Light (map pages 82, 85) is a beautiful and popular vantage point overlooking the lower portion of Pleasant Bay, the inlet separating the long, slender spits of North Beach and South Beach, and the Atlantic Ocean beyond. The view alone is worth the stop, but the birding potential is quite good as well. Check for gulls in any season, terns during the warmer months, and waterfowl in the winter. Large flocks of Common Eiders are present here some years. During the early spring and again in the fall, Northern Gannets can often be spotted, at times in spectacular concentrations, fishing off the outer beach or occasionally in the inlet itself. From late July through October, Parasitic Jaegers frequently wander into the inlet to harass the feeding terns, and the sharp-eyed observer may pick out a few shearwaters plying the distant horizon. During the late fall, Bonaparte's Gulls can be numerous and may be accompanied by a Black-headed Gull or Little Gull.

The **Chatham Fish Pier** (map page 82), off Shore Road, is worth a quick check in the winter for waterfowl and gulls, including an occasional Lesser Black-backed, Iceland, or Glaucous gull. The small island directly across from the pier is Tern Island, once the site of a large tern colony until an invasion of rats many years ago drove them out. Recently, dredge spoil from the harbor has been deposited on the island in hopes of attracting terns and Piping Plovers back to the island. Park in the upper parking lot (the lower lot is restricted to fishermen) and walk down to the fish packing building on the pier where a second-story observation deck is available to visitors.

Pleasant Bay (map page 82) hosts large numbers of wintering waterfowl including Great Cormorant, Brant, Common Eider, Bufflehead, Common Goldeneye (rarely a Barrow's), Red-breasted Merganser, and gulls. Check over the islands in the bay for a hunting Red-tailed Hawk, Northern Harrier or, rarely, a Bald Eagle. There are several public vantage points for checking the bay. Southernmost is the Cow Yard, off Harbor Road; at low tide, the flats here attract a few shorebirds during migration and gulls in any season. Other vantages are at the ends of Scateree Road and Cotchpinicut Road in Chathamport, and the end of Strong Island Road in North Chatham. Western portions of the bay can be checked from pull-offs on Route 28 in the towns of Harwich (at the intersection of Route 28 and Bay Road) and Orleans (north of the intersection of Route 28 and Tar Kiln Road).

Frost Fish Creek (map page 82), a small tidal creek that crosses under Route 28, is often worth a quick look during the winter or migration season. The flock of domestic Mallards and hybrids on the east side of the road sometimes attracts a wayward Wood Duck, Green-winged Teal, Northern Pintail, or American Wigeon during winter freeze-up. A short, narrow dirt drive on the west side of Route 28 (on the south side of the creek) provides access to conservation land (unmarked) where a trail runs between the creek and a wooded hillside. Gadwall and teal are possible on the creek and a few migrant songbirds may be present in season.

Lovers Lake (map page 82) usually attracts a variety of pond ducks during the winter, often including Pied-billed Grebe, American Wigeon, Ring-necked Duck, Lesser Scaup, Hooded Merganser, and American Coot; one or two Eurasian Wigeon have been present in some winters. Lovers Lake can be accessed from the end of Olde Town Lane, a private way whose owners have been tolerant of birders (please use appropriate discretion and courtesy).

Crows Pond (map page 82) is another good spot to look for waterfowl during the winter. You can check the pond from a pull-off on Seapine Road or the town landing on Fox Hill Road.

ORLEANS

The town of Orleans, "the gateway to the lower Cape," has become a very busy area but still offers some little-trampled sites for good fall, winter, and spring birding. Because of its location at the end of the Sandwich Moraine, the "backbone" of the Cape, Orleans is characterized by knob and kettle topography including kettle ponds, upland woods, and salt marshes.

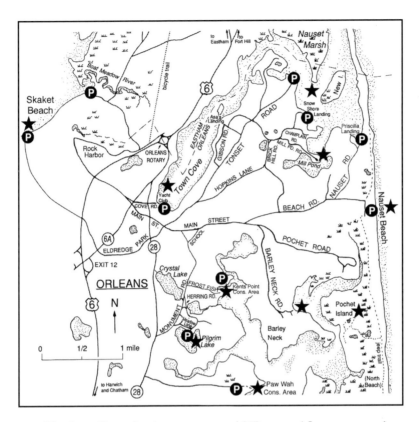

Skaket Beach (map page 103) provides expansive views of Cape Cod Bay. When brisk northerly winds blow in the fall, thousands of scoters, eiders, and other sea ducks can be seen migrating past, and this is an excellent spot to look for pelagic birds during and after northeasterly storms in the fall and winter (best conditions and species potential similar to First Encounter Beach in Eastham; page 109). The extensive tidal flats at low tide host a variety of shorebirds during migration, and, from late fall through spring, hundreds of Brant may be present. Check the gulls for Lesser Black-backed Gull.

Town Cove (map page 103) is a fine birding spot from late fall through early spring. A number of wintering waterfowl can be expected, typically including Great Cormorants, Brant, Black Ducks, Common Goldeneyes, rarely a Barrow's Goldeneye, Buffleheads, and Red-breasted Mergansers. Other species are possible, particularly when freshwater ponds have frozen. Great Blue Herons can be seen along the shore year-round, and other heron species may be present during the warmer months.

One of the best locations for checking the cove is the Orleans Yacht Club parking lot at the end of Cove Road (east off Route 28). The western edge of the cove just north of the parking lot contains a few springs that remain open through the most severe cold, attracting wintering Wilson's Snipe, Killdeer, and a variety of waterfowl. The small salt marsh behind the parking lot can be productive also; check the trees along the edge for perched raptors. Other good vantage points for Town Cove include the parking lot behind the Goose Hummock Shop on Route 6A and Asa's Landing off Gibson Road.

Nauset Marsh (map pages 103, 108) lies within the boundaries of the towns of Eastham and Orleans. It can be viewed from several vantages in East Orleans, including the end of Tonset Road, Snow Shore Landing, and Priscilla Landing. During the warmer months, expect to see herons, terns, gulls, and, at low tide, a variety of shorebirds. In the winter, Great Cormorants, Brant, Common Eiders, a variety of other waterfowl, gulls, and an occasional raptor may be present.

A short distance to the north of Priscilla Landing lies New Island, which was once the southern tip of Coast Guard Beach. It was created when the ocean severed the beach in the late 1970s (and is thus not so "new" anymore!). For most of the 1980s and 1990s, the island hosted a large colony of nesting terns and Laughing Gulls, but heavy predation by Great Horned Owls and others led to its eventual abandonment. The island also used to be excellent for roosting shorebirds at high tide, but the majority of birds now roost on Coast Guard Beach to the north (page 112).

Snow Shore Landing and Priscilla Landing are both good sites from which to launch a kayak or canoe to more fully explore the entire Nauset ecosystem. A less strenuous way to bird this area is to take one of the popular Nauset Marsh cruises conducted by Mass Audubon's Wellfleet Bay Wildlife Sanctuary. These trips are about three hours in duration and cover not only New Island but also other destinations in the southern part of the marsh. These excursions are thoroughly enjoyable with great birding. Contact the Sanctuary (page 113) for a schedule, (508) 349-2615.

Harlequin Ducks

Mill Pond (map page 103), accessible from the end of Mill Pond Road, has mussel flats that, when exposed at low tide, attract a variety of shorebirds including yellowlegs, dowitchers, plovers, and "peeps." Occasionally, a Snowy Egret or two will fly in to chase minnows.

Nauset Beach (map page 103) is an excellent spot to look for seabirds from October through April. Through the years this has been the best location on the Cape to find Harlequin Ducks; some winters, as many as a dozen have been present. King Eider has also been found here from time to time. The best spot to find both of these species is a couple of hundred yards north of the parking lot. Among the more common species that are likely to be present are Common and Red-throated loons, Horned and Red-necked grebes, all three species of scoters, Common Eiders, and Red-breasted Mergansers. In the spring and fall, gannets pass by regularly, sometimes by the hundreds, and in winter alcids, most often Razorbills, may appear. Check the beach and small marsh to the north for the occasional Northern Harrier or falcon. A walk through the dunes in the winter may turn up the "Ipswich" form of the Savannah Sparrow, Snow Buntings, or, if you're very lucky, a Snowy Owl.

Pochet Island (map page 103), one of the least-known yet most beautiful spots on the Cape, offers fine birding from fall through spring. Access is limited to those with four-wheel-drive vehicles or the energy to hike a mile or so down the beach. This has kept the privately owned island a virtual sanctuary. A well-kept system of trails covers the island, which has several small swampy areas and one small pond. Most of the island is covered with a dense growth of shrubs and brambles, but there are also several groves of pines. During migration a wide variety of migrant passerines and hawks are attracted to this oasis. In the winter, check the pine groves for owls and keep an eye on the sky for hawks. The bluff at the south end of the island affords the quiet birder a look at waterfowl feeding in the marsh below, as well as one of the most spectacular vistas imaginable.

Pochet Island is deserted during most of the year. The island's seasonal residents have been very accommodating and welcome most visitors. Please respect their privacy. To reach Pochet, park at the Nauset Beach parking lot and hike south on the beach-buggy trail for a mile or so to the island. A small bridge across a tidal creek provides access (during extreme high tides, part of the trail may be underwater). Even if there are few birds to be found, a hike to Pochet is well worth the effort.

The end of **Barley Neck Road** (map page 103) offers a view of the back side of Pochet Island and the estuary separating the island from the mainland. Watch for hawks over the island and a variety of waterfowl on the water or tucked into the marshy edges, occasionally including wintering Green-winged Teal and American Wigeons. Eurasian Wigeons have been found here in the past.

Pilgrim Lake (map page 103) is another good duck pond, which can be viewed in part from the town beach at the end of Herring Brook Way. Look for Pied-billed Grebe, American Wigeon (rarely a Eurasian Wigeon), Ring-necked Duck, scaup, Hooded Merganser, and American Coot among others.

The **Kent's Point Conservation Area** (map page 103), located off Frost Fish Lane (dirt; follow the signs), is on a wooded peninsula jutting into The River, the northernmost extension of Pleasant Bay. In winter, there is usually open water here because of the strong tidal currents in this area, and duck watching at this season can be very productive. Great Horned Owls usually nest somewhere on the property, and a modest variety of songbirds in the pine woodlands may include nuthatches, Brown Creeper, and Pine Warbler. A kiosk at the parking lot has a map of the area, and a map can also be downloaded from the town web site: www.town.orleans.ma.us/.

The **Paw Wah Point Conservation Area** (map page 103), located near the end of Namequoit Road in South Orleans (watch for the signs), provides access to the northern shore of Little Pleasant Bay. A trail makes a loop from the small parking area through pine woodlands to a vantage point over the bay and to Hog and Sampson Islands to the east. During the winter, waterfowl are numerous, while in the warmer months Osprey nest on a platform between the two islands.

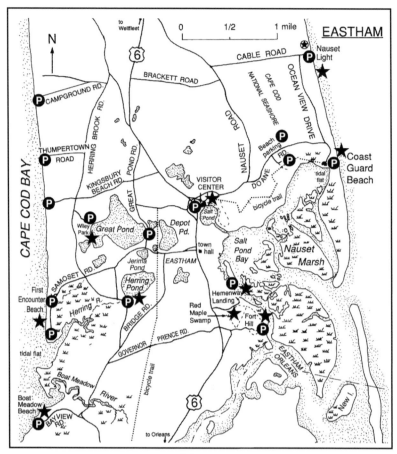

EASTHAM

The town of Eastham has some of the top birding spots on the Cape. The topography ranges from the low rolling hills in the southern part of the town to the higher Eastham plains area around Nauset Light. The Cape Cod National Seashore has preserved many acres of prime habitat in the town.

Boat Meadow Beach (map page 108), a small dirt parking area at the end of Bayview Road, provides another access point to the southeastern corner of Cape Cod Bay. It lies just to the south of First Encounter Beach (page 109) and the birding prospects are similar, though somewhat more limited. Public access to Cape

Cod Bay is also available from town beaches at the ends of Kingsbury Beach Road, Thumpertown Road, Campground Road, and South Sunken Meadow Road.

First Encounter Beach (map page 108) is renowned as a place for land-based observations of pelagic birds during and immediately following storms. Prime conditions typically consist of strong, clearing, northwest winds following close on the heels of a coastal northeast storm, as the seabirds blown into Cape Cod Bay by the storm stream past the beach in their attempt to find a route back out to the open ocean. However, even ideal conditions do not guarantee a good show; conversely, seemingly unfavorable conditions can occasionally result in some surprising sightings. August through December is the most productive time, but any season offers some possibilities. A general rule is "if in doubt, check it out!"

The list of potential species at this vantage point reads like a who's who of oceanic wanderers, including shearwaters, storm-petrels, gannets, jaegers, kittiwakes, alcids, loons, and all of the sea ducks. Such rarities as Sabine's Gull, Long-tailed Jaeger, and Great Skua have been seen here with some regularity.

The area has much to offer aside from the possibility of seeing pelagics. Shorebirds, gulls, and terns frequent the extensive tidal flats from May through November. Saltmarsh Sharp-tailed Sparrows nest in the marsh, where herons are often present as well. In the fall falcons regularly pass, and in the late fall to early winter Snow Buntings and Lapland Longspurs can be found (most often at the far end of the parking lot).

Great Pond and **Herring Pond** (map page 108) are two of the most productive freshwater ponds on the outer Cape. Pied-billed Grebe, Mute Swan, American Wigeon (rarely a Eurasian Wigeon), Ring-necked Duck, Lesser Scaup, Hooded Merganser, Ruddy Duck, and

American Coot are among the more regular species. Great Pond can be checked from the public parking lot off Great Pond Road (best light in the morning) and from Wiley Park off Herring Brook Road (best light in the afternoon). Herring Pond can be easily viewed from the town landing off Herring Brook Road. Jemima Pond, at the intersection of Samoset Road and Great Pond Road, often has Hooded Mergansers.

Fort Hill (map page 108) is one of the premier birding locales in the entire state, and affords a magnificent vista over Nauset Marsh and Bay, Coast Guard Beach, and the distant ocean. The grassy fields, mowed periodically by the Cape Cod National Seashore, are among the last remnants of what was once the predominant habitat on Cape Cod. The birding prospects are rich and varied throughout the year, though from late summer through early winter is perhaps the most exciting time.

The fields here are the only known breeding site on Cape Cod for Bobolinks, though they may not nest here every year. In the spring, the field edges are good places to witness the dusk flight displays of American Woodcocks. During the fall, migrant sparrows may be common, and the thickets and wooded edges often harbor a few warblers or other songbirds. The dense tangles of multiflora rose attract Northern Mockingbirds and other wintering frugivores. When the tide is running abnormally high (11 feet or more in Boston) during the fall and winter, the marsh floods completely, forcing American Bitterns, rails (Virginia and Clapper are the most likely), Saltmarsh Sharp-tailed Sparrows, Nelson's Sharp-tailed Sparrows, and Seaside Sparrows up into the thickets and dense grass at the base of the hill. The small creek and swampy depression on the southwestern corner of the hill also attract migrant and wintering rails, herons, and waterfowl. Hawks are seen frequently, except in midsummer, and small flights are recorded regularly during migration, particularly in the spring. This is one of the best spots on the Cape for Northern Shrike in flight years.

The extensive marsh attracts high numbers of birds year-round including herons, waterfowl, shorebirds, terns, and gulls. Great Blue Herons are almost always present, counts in the fall sometimes exceeding 100 individuals. During the warmer months, Snowy and Great Egrets, and Green-backed Herons are generally conspicuous, and a Tricolored Heron or Yellow-crowned Night-Heron is possible, especially in the late summer. Shorebirds are numerous in May and again from July through November, though often they are too distant to identify easily. A few may roost during high tide in the small tidal pools at the base of the hill. During the colder months, flocks of Brant, Canada Geese, Black Ducks, and Red-breasted Mergansers appear. In midwinter, when the freshwater ponds freeze over, other species of waterfowl, such as Hooded and Common mergansers, may be present.

The **Red Maple Swamp** (map page 108), located off the road that leads to Fort Hill, is a lovely area but usually rather quiet birdwise. A trail and boardwalk wind through this dark, swampy woodland where mosses and catbrier drape over large twisted maples and tupelos. In the spring and fall you may encounter a few migrant passerines here. Access is from the lower parking lot at Fort Hill or from Hemenway Landing.

Hemenway Landing (map page 108), off Route 6 just to the north of Fort Hill, affords another view of the Nauset Marsh system. At low tide, the exposed flats attract shorebirds and other species, but many are distant and difficult to identify. Herons are present in the marsh during the warmer months and are most conspicuous late in the day when they begin traveling to and from their roosts. During the fall and winter, raptors and a variety of waterfowl may be seen here. This is also a good spot for launching canoes and kayaks to explore the Nauset Marsh system.

The **Salt Pond Visitor Center** (map page 108) of the Cape Cod National Seashore has a variety of exhibits providing an overview of the natural history of the area and is worth a stop for the visiting birder. Salt Pond usually has a handful of herons, ducks, shorebirds, and gulls in season. Foot and bicycle trails lead from the visitor center out along the northern edge of Nauset Marsh, ending eventually at Coast Guard Beach. Several spots along the trails offer good views of the marsh and tidal flats. Prairie Warblers nest in the red cedars throughout this area.

Coast Guard Beach (map page 108) is another of the foremost birding locales on the outer Cape. From the bluff in front of the old Coast Guard station it is possible to scan the ocean for shearwaters (infrequent), gannets, sea ducks, terns, kittiwakes, and alcids in season. The tidal flats below the parking lot are packed with shorebirds from July through November as well as a variety of herons, waterfowl, gulls, and terns. The largest concentrations occur a couple of hours before high tide when most of the flats elsewhere in the marsh have become submerged. Most numerous are Black-bellied and Semipalmated plovers, Greater and Lesser yellowlegs, Semipalmated and Least sandpipers, Dunlins, and Short-billed Dowitchers. Forster's Terns are regular during the late summer and early fall. A walk down the beach during the summer will produce Piping Plovers (several pairs typically nest here) and Least Terns. At high tide hundreds to thousands of shorebirds, primarily "peeps" and Semipalmated Plovers, roost on the inside edge of the southern tip. Large flocks of terns are also present during the late summer. Ospreys nest on the platforms in the marsh, and during the fall keep an eye out for passing Peregrine Falcons, Merlins, and Northern Harriers. From late fall into the winter, Snow Buntings and Lapland Longspurs may be found in the dunes, and in flight years Snowy Owls are possible.

During the off-season, you can park in the lot behind the old Coast Guard station, but in the summer you must park at the Little Creek lot off Doane Road and take the shuttle bus to the beach. Another option is to park at the Doane Rock parking lot, on the south side of Doane Road; park at the far (east) end of the lower lot and follow the trail to the bicycle trail that runs along the northern end of Nauset Marsh before reaching the base of Coast Guard Beach (just below the old Coast Guard station). Much of the beach is off-limits during the breeding season in order to protect the nesting birds, so heed the posted signs.

Nauset Light Beach (map page 108), part of the Cape Cod National Seashore, is another good vantage point from which to scope the ocean, offering the possibility for a variety of the typical oceanic species in season.

WELLFLEET

Wellfleet is dominated by its harbor and associated salt marshes and tidal flats. The uplands are a mix of pitch pine and oak woods and open bearberry heath. Freshwater kettle ponds cover an extensive area, as do the Herring River Valley and its associated freshwater wetlands and floodplain. Much of the town lies within the protected boundaries of the Cape Cod National Seashore. Wellfleet has something to offer the birder year-round, with several "must-visit" areas.

Mass Audubon's **Wellfleet Bay Wildlife Sanctuary** (map page 114) is the first stop as you enter Wellfleet from the south on Route 6. This 1,100-acre sanctuary is a microcosm of the Cape in the variety of habitats that are found there. The pitch pine-oak woods, open fields,

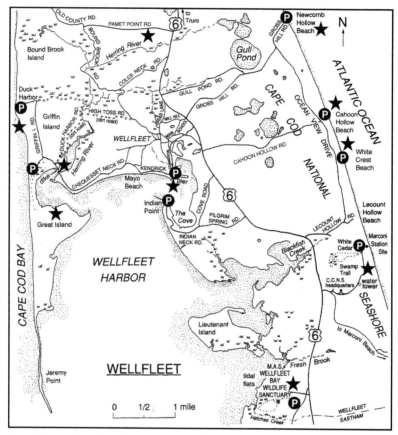

heathlands, freshwater ponds, salt marshes, tidal flats, and beaches offer a wide range of birding opportunities. All seasons can be productive. There is an entry fee for non-members.

In the spring, the best birding is along the Silver Spring Trail, which skirts a freshwater pond created by the damming of Silver Spring Brook. This is one of the better warbler spots on the Cape—as many as 25 species have been seen in one day, though such a total is now very unlikely—and several of the rarer southern species have been seen here with some regularity. In addition, a number of other passerines including flycatchers, thrushes, vireos, tanagers, orioles, and sparrows may be found in the trees and thickets surrounding the pond. Wood Ducks are occasionally present on the pond.

Snow Bunting

Summer and fall, and spring to a lesser degree, are the best times to see shorebirds at the sanctuary. By following the Goose Pond Trail, you will reach Goose Pond, several salt marsh tide pools beyond, and eventually the beach, all good areas for shorebirds and herons. Patient perusal of the edges of the Goose Pond may produce a Virginia Rail or Sora during the fall.

The best time to bird the tidal flats, which are reached by following the Goose Pond Trail past Try Island and taking the boardwalk across the marsh, is on an incoming tide, one to three hours after low tide. At that time the birds are close to the marsh and beach rather than spread out over the extensive flats. In the late summer and fall, in addition to the numerous shorebirds, Common, Roseate, Least, Forster's, and Black terns often are present on the flats. Of special interest are the Whimbrels, which frequent the marsh to feed on fiddler crabs during July and August. During the day, a dozen or more birds can be seen, but as evening approaches their numbers swell as birds from elsewhere gather before departing for roosting areas to the south; counts as high as 200 have been recorded at this time.

In addition to the trails, the Esther Underwood Johnson Nature Center offers an excellent bird feeding station, informative exhibits about local wildlife, and a gift/book shop. Numerous natural history programs for adults, families, and children are offered year-round. These programs include guided bird walks, birding tours, boat trips, and field classes. Contact the Sanctuary for schedules and details (P.O. Box 236, South Wellfleet, MA 02663; telephone: 508-349-2615; email: wellfleet@mass-audubon.org; web site: www.wellfleetbay.org).

The **Marconi Station** (map page 114) area of the Cape Cod National Seashore is located just north of the Wellfleet Bay Wildlife Sanctuary on the east side of Route 6. The road into the site goes through a sparsely vege-tated area where Horned Larks nest. This is one of the last areas on the Cape where Vesper Sparrows still breed; look for them around the headquarters building and along the road out toward the water tower. During the fall migration, a variety of sparrows can generally be found here, often including rarer species such as Lark, Clay-colored, or Grasshopper sparrows. It is also a good area to look for wintering Eastern Bluebirds. The obser-vation deck at the Marconi Station is one of the better hawk-watching sites on the Cape, both in spring and fall, and the ocean overlook provides a great vantage to scope for seabirds. The White Cedar Swamp Trail typi-cally has few birds during the day, but at night the intrepid birder may be rewarded with a calling Northern Saw-whet Owl or Eastern Screech-Owl, both of which have nested here. Whip-poor-wills are also resident during the summer, and in recent years Chuck-will'swidows have become regular and may be nesting; both species can often be heard at dusk from mid-May through July.

LeCount Hollow Beach, White Crest Beach, Cahoon Hollow Beach, and **Newcomb Hollow Beach** (map page 114) all provide good views of the ocean and the possibility of finding gannets, sea ducks, gulls, terns, and occasionally pelagics.

Wellfleet Harbor (map page 114), accessible from the town pier off Commercial Street, offers fine birding from late October into early January. During this time the birder is likely to see Red-throated and Common loons, Horned Grebes, Brant, eiders, Oldsquaws, and scoters. Laughing Gulls, Bonaparte's Gulls, and lingering terns are typically present during this season as well, and Common Black-headed Gulls have turned up with some regularity. Alcids also may be seen, particularly after storms; check around the pier for Dovekies, Razorbills, or murres.

Another good spot for checking Wellfleet Harbor is from Indian Point at the end of Indian Neck Road. The open area at the end of the road is a good place to look for Horned Larks, Snow Buntings, and sparrows, and a few shorebirds and gulls often roost on the breakwater at high tide.

The **Chequessett Neck Road Dike** (map page 114) is a good spot to check in any season. The Herring River flows under the dike and is often one of the few areas of open water in winter when everything else has frozen. At low tide, in season, a few shorebirds, herons, and gulls feed in the shallow water. Laughing Gulls, Bonaparte's Gulls, and terns are often present during the fall. At high tide in the spring and fall, ducks, predominantly Black Ducks and Mallards, come into this area to feed, giving the birder a good close look. In recent years, especially in the fall, as many as three or four Ospreys have been seen, just after the tide turns, feeding on menhaden and white perch.

Duck Harbor Road, the dirt road running north along the west side of the river, and High Toss Road, which branches off to the right, can be good places to find migrant passerines and hawks. The junction of the two roads, where High Toss Road crosses the river, is one of the most productive spots. Virginia Rail and Sora are possible here during migration. The open areas can be good for Northern Shrike in flight years. Duck Harbor Road is closed to vehicle traffic, but it is possible to park at the south end of Duck Harbor Road or the east end of High Toss Road and walk in.

Great Island (map page 114) offers good birding potential for the ambitious birder willing to do some hiking. A well-marked trail runs south from the parking lot near the end of Chequessett Neck Road, providing access to the island, as well as Wellfleet Harbor to the east and Cape Cod Bay to the west. The rigorous hike is likely to produce a good variety and number of waterfowl during the colder months, shorebirds and terns from late spring through early fall, a variety of gulls year-round, migrant and wintering raptors, and a few songbird migrants in the pine woodlands in the fall.

Duck Harbor (map page 114), the beach at the end of Griffin Island Road, is a good winter birding spot. Red-necked Grebes, eiders, scoters, goldeneyes, and Red-breasted Mergansers are likely here.

Pamet Point Road (map page 114), which runs west from Route 6, lies entirely within the bounds of the Cape Cod National Seashore and traverses some relatively undisturbed pine-oak woodland. A walk along the road in May or June will yield a good variety of nesting songbirds, including Eastern Wood-Pewee, Great Crested Flycatcher, White-breasted and Red-breasted nuthatches, Red-eyed Vireo, Brown Creeper, Hermit Thrush, Pine and Black-and-white warblers, Ovenbird, Scarlet Tanager, Eastern Towhee, and Baltimore Oriole. May also offers a good chance for migrant vireos, warblers, and others, particularly along the western portions where the largest oaks line the road. Park anywhere along the road where there is adequate room to pull off.

TRURO

Truro, the smallest town on Cape Cod, is characterized by pitch pine woods and rolling bearberry moors, intersected by old outwash valleys such as the Pamet River Valley and Longnook Valley. The town, which has avoided most of the commercial development so evident elsewhere on the Cape, provides several locations to view the ocean and Cape Cod Bay, a good selection of pine-barrens breeding species, and some good sites for viewing migrating hawks and other migrants. A large portion of the town has been protected within the Cape Cod National Seashore.

Prince Valley Road (map page 120) runs west from Route 6 through relatively undisturbed pine-oak woodland (much of it within the bounds of the National Seashore land) providing good access to breeding species such as Whip-poor-will, Eastern Wood-Pewee, Great Crested Flycatcher, Red-breasted Nuthatch, Brown Creeper, Hermit Thrush, Pine Warbler, Ovenbird, and Eastern Towhee. During May, pockets of migrant warblers are possible, particularly where oaks predominate. There are several places where you can pull off on the side of the road, park, then bird by foot along the roadside.

Pamet Harbor (map page 120) has sanded in rather badly in recent years and has deteriorated as a birding spot but is still worth a quick look if you're in the neighborhood. A few shorebirds and terns utilize the sandy flats during the warmer months while a few ducks and gulls are usually present during the colder months. The flats on nearby Mill Pond Road, when exposed, often host

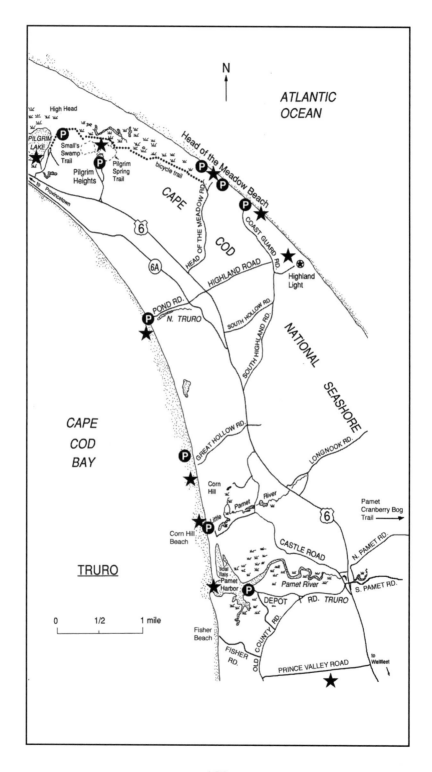

a few shorebirds in the fall, occasionally including an American Golden-Plover or Pectoral Sandpiper; the flats can be checked from the shoulder of Mill Pond Road.

The **Pamet Cranberry Bog Trail** (map page 120), a Cape Cod National Seashore trail at the end of North Pamet Road, leads to a small cranberry bog and traverses some prime heathland habitat. A small dirt parking lot on the south side of the road, adjacent to the Truro NEED Center (National Environmental Education Development Collaborative) housed in an old Coast Guard building, provides access to the trail on the north side of the road. The more wooded portions of the trail leading down to the bog can harbor a few migrant songbirds in season, while the highest sections traverse extensive bearberry barrens, where expansive panoramas can be great for viewing migrating raptors.

The **Cape Cod Bay** (map page 120) shoreline of Truro is likely to yield many sea ducks during migration and winter. At times, thousands of Red-breasted Mergansers have amassed here, and Northern Gannets can occur in impressive concentrations during spring and fall movements. Pelagics are possible as well, especially after northeasterly storms. Access points for viewing the bay include Ryder Beach at the end of Ryder Beach Road, Fisher Beach at the end of Fisher Road, Corn Hill Beach off Corn Hill Road (the dunes south of the parking lot are good for Northern Harrier, Horned Lark, Lapland Longspur, and Snow Bunting in season), Great Hollow Beach at the end of Great Hollow Road, and the parking lot at the end of Pond Road in North Truro.

Ballston Beach at the end of South Pamet Road, **Longnook Beach** at the end of Longnook Road, and **Coast Guard Beach** (not to be confused with the same named beach in Eastham) at the end of Coast Guard Road (map page 120) are good locations to check the ocean for migrant and wintering sea ducks and the occasional pelagic species.

Highland Light (map page 120) is a good hawk-watching site, particularly in the spring. Park in the small parking area in front of the lighthouse and watch for hawks approaching from the south.

Head of the Meadow Beach (map page 120) has been the most productive of the ocean-side beaches in Truro, affording a good chance for loons, gannets, sea ducks, gulls, alcids (primarily Razorbills), and occasionally shearwaters, storm-petrels, and jaegers in season. The bicycle trail at the north end of the parking lot runs north between the marsh and pine barrens, ending at Pilgrim Lake. It can be well worth exploring, particularly during migration, for land birds, hawks, and marsh birds, and affords a pleasant walk in any season. There are two parking lots: the southern provides the best view of the water but is town owned and requires a resident parking sticker in the summer; the northern lot is part of the National Seashore and is accessible in any season, though a fee is charged during the summer. Seasonal restrooms are available.

The **Pilgrim Heights** (map page 120) area is the Cape's premier spring hawk-watching site. The Cape narrows to its thinnest width here, funneling most of the raptors into easy viewing range. The Wellfleet Bay Wildlife Sanctuary has sponsored a systematic hawk watch here, documenting the passage of hundreds of raptors annually from late March through early June. In addition to raptors, many other diurnal migrants pass through the area, and, when the winds are favorable (i.e., out of the westerly quadrant), loons, swallows, blackbirds, and others can be expected. The patches of pines and oaks in the area, as well as Small Swamp itself, can harbor warblers, vireos, kinglets, thrushes, and other migrants from early April through early June.

Hawk-watching is best from the overlooks on the Small Swamp Trail, particularly the second, which is

Broad-winged Hawk

where the organized watch is conducted. If you bear right at the first fork in the trail, you will come to the first of two overlooks; continue down the trail a short distance and you will arrive at the second. The hawks appear out over the dunes, frequently right below the lookout, or they approach from over the woods to the southeast. They are often seen going both north, "outbound," as well as south on their return after reaching land's end in Provincetown. Most common are Turkey Vultures, Sharp-shinned Hawks, Broad-winged Hawks, and American Kestrels, with smaller numbers of Ospreys, Red-tailed Hawks, Merlins, and Northern Harriers. A Peregrine Falcon or Bald Eagle will occasionally spice up the day, and the site has proven to be by far the most reliable spot in all of New England for southern vagrants such as Mississippi Kite (now nearly annual) and Swallow-tailed Kite. Northern Harriers nest in the dunes nearby, and in the early spring the males can be seen performing their remarkable courtship flights. Unlike hawk watching at inland sites, the birds at Pilgrim Heights are seldom just dots in the sky but often pass at fairly close range, sometimes strikingly close—photographers bring your camera! Scoping the ocean may provide distant views of migrating Northern Gannets or the spouts of whales.

The bicycle trail that winds along the edge of the marsh below the bluff can be a good place to look for warblers and other passerines. Follow the Pilgrim Spring Trail (east from the kiosk) until you come to the paved bicycle trail, which you can take in either direction. Be mindful of bikers; they have the right of way. On a good migration day, the thickets of shadbush, blueberry, and winterberry along the edges of the trail can be productive for migrant songbirds. Maps of the area are available at the trailhead and at the Cape Cod National Seashore visitor centers in Eastham, South Wellfleet, and Provincetown. Restrooms (closed in winter) are located off the second parking lot.

Pilgrim Lake (map pages 120, 126) is gradually sanding in and, though historically a good birding location, hosts few birds these days. You can easily and quickly check it, however, by carefully pulling off Route 6 onto the sandy shoulder. During winter, the flocks of roosting gulls will often include one or more Iceland Gulls and, more rarely, a Lesser Black-backed Gull or Glaucous Gull. Ducks, aside from the ubiquitous Black Duck, are usually few, but Common Mergansers can be numerous in the winter, and a few scaup may be present as well. Attempts are currently underway to increase the tidal flow into the lake; time will tell how this will impact the lake's avifauna.

PROVINCETOWN

On a day-to-day basis, probably no other town on Cape Cod offers the birding potential of Provincetown, and the visiting birder would do well to allow at least a half-day for exploring this fascinating community. Composed entirely of sand washed northward from Cape Cod's eroding eastern shore and virtually surrounded by water, the town, along with its human and natural history, has been deeply sculpted by the sea. Almost every aspect of the area—the bird life, plant life, geology, and human culture—is remarkably unique and reflects the ocean's pervasive influence. Fortunately, much of the town lies within the protected confines of the Cape Cod National Seashore.

Appropriately for a community with such a strong marine heritage, there is probably no place in eastern North America that offers quite the potential for seeing pelagic birds. Although a few seabirds are generally present in any season, during the fall and early winter the concentrations can be spectacular. In the spring, migrating songbirds and hawks are funneled northward along the outer Cape and, reluctant to cross the water, become concentrated in Provincetown, often in large numbers. In the fall, the area provides the first landfall for migrants that have drifted off course over the Gulf of Maine. Only during the midsummer, when the avian population is low and the human population high, does the birding slow down, though even then the visiting birder will generally find something of interest.

The **Beech Forest** (map pages 126, 127), part of the Cape Cod National Seashore, is without a doubt the finest spot on Cape Cod to witness the spring passerine migration, and is also worth birding in the fall, particularly from late August through September when warblers are passing south. It is an oasis among the dunes, with small

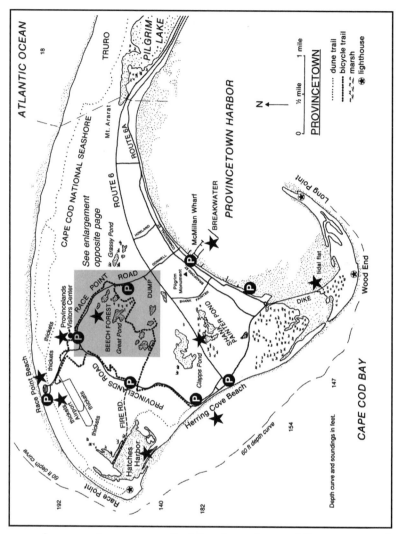

marshy ponds surrounded by beeches, alders, several species of pines, and most notably oaks. Those areas where oaks predominate are where you are most likely to encounter spring migrants, though fall migrants are more widespread and might be anywhere. Species to be expected include all of the typical eastern Massachusetts migrants; on a good day in the spring, it's possible to see 20 or more species of warblers. The following descriptions pertain primarily to the spring season when the location of the birds is more predictably associated with

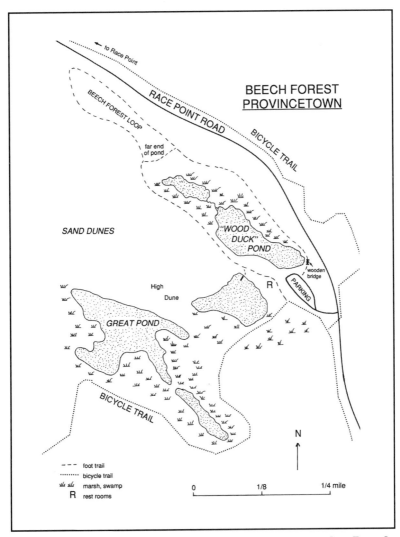

to Race Point

BEECH FOREST LOOP

RACE POINT ROAD

far end
of pond

BICYCLE TRAIL

**BEECH FOREST
PROVINCETOWN**

SAND DUNES

"WOOD
DUCK"
POND

wooden
bridge

High
Dune

R

PARKING

GREAT POND

BICYCLE TRAIL

N

- - - foot trail
········· bicycle trail
ᵂᵂ ᵂᵂ marsh, swamp
R   rest rooms

0   1/8   1/4 mile

specific habitats. Some of the better spots in the Beech Forest are the following.

Wooden Bridge: This area adjacent to the parking lot is among the most consistently productive. If any birds are around at all, there is likely to be a pocket of them here. Check the oaks on the opposite side of Race Point Road as well.

Far End of "Wood Duck" Pond: The trail in this section, with its large oaks and beeches, is the most consistently productive, particularly early in the morning.

It is sheltered from most of the raw ocean breezes and catches the warmth of the rising sun. Several "layers" of birding potential are present here, from the moist, swampy hollow below to the neck-stiffening tops of the highest trees on the hillside above. On a good day it can be difficult to decide whether to look up, down, or straight ahead!

"High Dune": This is one of the better locations in Provincetown to see spring hawks. To reach it, watch for a section of split-rail fence on the south side of the main trail. Turn south here, away from "Wood Duck" Pond, and follow the sandy trail through the scrub pine to the highest vantage point. A clear view is available in all directions, and most of the town can be seen. It seems that sooner or later most of the hawks present in the area on a given day will pass by this dune as they mill about, and the birder is often afforded excellent eye-level views. All of the common raptors of the Northeast can be expected here, and some of the accidental southern species, such as Mississippi and Swallow-tailed kites, have been recorded as well.

Other spots in the Beech Forest worth checking for migrants are the bicycle trail on the northeast side of Race Point Road, the oaks at the northwest corner of the forest, the main trail from the split rail fence to the restrooms, and the bicycle trail from the restrooms south between the ponds (though this can be partially underwater during wet springs). During weekend afternoons the parking lot and main trail can become cluttered with weekenders who are often noisy and can hamper birding efforts; try to arrive early, when the birding is best anyway, to beat the rush. Access to the parking lot is off Race Point Road.

The **Province Lands Visitor Center** (map page 126) of the Cape Cod National Seashore sits on a high bluff, with spectacular views over the northern portions of town, and is another good place to see hawks. Watch from the parking lot or, better still, go to the observation deck at the top of the building from which the outer dunes can be scanned for falcons and accipiters. Seasonal restrooms are available here.

The **Provincetown Municipal Airport** (map page 126) and vicinity is mainly of interest in the fall when the many thickets attract numerous passerines, and accipiters and falcons frequently pass over. Park at the Race Point Beach parking lot and walk back to the airport (the airport parking lot is reserved for customers). From here you can proceed southwest following the line of wet thickets that extend from the parking lot to the end of the runway; keep well away from the runway. If you are

Dovekies

ambitious and continue far enough—about 1.25 miles—you will end up at Hatches Harbor (page 133). On a good day the complete route, although arduous, is well worth the effort. An alternative is to walk down the outer beach from the Race Point Beach parking lot and walk back along the airport; this loop combines the possibilities of seeing both seabirds and land birds.

Race Point (map page 126) is one of the finest locations in eastern North America to watch for seabirds, with the potential for a diverse and exciting array of pelagics, particularly from late August through February. All of the regular northwest Atlantic pelagics have been seen here, and the more common species are seen with some regularity and occasionally in large numbers when conditions are favorable.

Exactly why these birds occur with such consistency in this vicinity remains uncertain, though a variety of factors are likely to be involved. Undoubtedly, Provincetown's location, thrusting prominently toward the Gulf of Maine, results in many seabirds being intercepted by this land mass as they move southward during the fall. The rich Stellwagen Bank, host to an abundance of marine birds and mammals, lies just a few miles to the north and certainly contributes to many of the sightings from land. Another important factor appears to be the presence of deep (100+ feet) water close to shore in this area. Presumably, this sharp drop-off results in some upwelling and, in conjunction with the strong rips and currents characteristic of the region, provides a source of plentiful food. This deep-water line can be seen from the Race Point Beach parking lot (at the end of Province Lands Road), if the sea is fairly calm, some 800 yards out from shore where the shallow, light blue water turns to a deep, dark blue. Farther to the west this line occurs progressively closer to shore and is closest, roughly 200 yards away, just north of the tip of Race Point itself (see map page 126).

Generally, the best weather conditions for producing birds at Race Point consist of cloudy skies with light to moderate northeast winds, although during the peak season, late August to November, a few birds can usually be found under most any conditions. When the winds are strong (exceeding 40 miles per hour) from the northeast, viewing is very difficult particularly if it is raining. The dunes in front of the parking lot have built up, making it is nearly impossible to see the water from the comfort of a car, making it necessary to brave the elements. The old Coast Guard station just to the east of the parking lot can afford some protection from the weather. (Viewing pelagics from land is rarely a comfortable endeavor in any location!)

Strong northwest winds following a northeast storm can provide a good show as the pelagics that were blown into Cape Cod Bay by the storm stream back out into the open ocean. During the warmer months, fog may cause a few pelagics to drift in close to land; but you must be on hand at the moment the fog clears because little if anything can be seen before and the birds move out rapidly as visibility improves. Be forewarned that the ocean here can be as barren as anywhere; finding pelagics is always a hit-or-miss proposition.

This is one of the best places in the Northeast from which to see jaegers from land. Numbers are highly variable from year to year, but often from mid-August through October, with a little patience and a sharp eye, you can see at least one or two jaegers, and, at times, counts of a dozen or more are possible. The Parasitic Jaeger is by far the most common species, but Pomarine Jaegers are seen from time to time (primarily after storms) and Long-tailed Jaeger is reported very rarely. You may also see impressive numbers of shearwaters; counts in the hundreds and even thousands are not uncommon in some years, especially after storms. Greater Shearwater is the predominant species, but Sooty Shearwater is also possible, particularly in the early summer; and, during the summer and early fall of some years, Cory's Shearwater can be found. From August through October, this is an excellent spot to look for Manx Shearwaters as well.

When conditions are favorable, meaning light winds (ideally out of the east or southeast), a walk from the

Greater Shearwater

parking lot west out to Race Point itself can be unsurpassed for close observations of pelagics from land. Deep water is less than 200 yards offshore at the point, and shearwaters, terns, gulls, alcids, and others are often present at remarkably close range. During the winter months, murres, Razorbills, and guillemots are likely and, if seas are calm, often can be seen sitting and feeding along the deep-water line. Walking out to the point involves a rigorous, four-mile hike (round-trip) through soft sand but can be very rewarding on the right days.

While looking for birds in this area, keep an eye out for spouting whales, which are present throughout the year with the largest numbers generally occurring during the spring and fall. Typically, fin and humpback whales are the most common, but minke and northern right whales are possible and white-sided dolphins are seen on occasion. "Have you seen any whales?" is a question often posed to the scope-wielding birder. Seasonal restrooms are available at the parking lot.

Hatches Harbor (map page 126), as its name indicates, once served as a harbor but has now sanded in, a fate to which every body of water in Provincetown seems destined. This "harbor" now consists of a small patch of salt marsh and some tidal flats, separated from the bay by a spit of sand. On the east it is bordered by a dike; to the east of the dike lies the airport with its border of wet thickets. The flats and spit attract large numbers of gulls year-round and terns from July to October, and occasionally the rarer members of their clan can be found. Iceland Gull and Lesser Black-backed Gull can be found here with some regularity. A few shorebirds are also usually present in season. Harbor seals frequently haul out on the spit during the winter. Although the habitat is limited here, the "land's-end" location makes it the type of spot where almost anything might drop in. Access is by foot from the Race Point Beach parking lot, Herring Cove, or a small, unmarked, dirt parking lot on the west side of Province Lands Road (the southernmost of two lots), about a mile south of the National Seashore Visitor center. From this latter parking lot, a dirt fire road runs northwest to the dike separating Hatches Harbor from the airport, and provides the shortest (though not necessarily the most productive for seeing birds) hike to both the harbor and Race Point.

Herring Cove (map page 126) is another vantage point for viewing seabirds, but, because the observer is at a low elevation and the birds are usually at a considerable distance from shore, it is generally less productive than the Race Point area (which is visible to the north). Poor light can also be a problem during the afternoon. Large numbers of terns feed there from late summer to early fall and often attract jaegers into easy viewing range. Various sea ducks are common during the colder months, and the begging gulls on the beach may be joined by an Iceland Gull or Lesser Black-backed Gull.

Shank Painter Pond (map page 126) is one of those places that looks as if it should be full of birds yet rarely produces anything. Wood Ducks or Green-winged Teal are sometimes present during the warmer months, but otherwise there is little to be said about the area. It is easy to check from Route 6, however, and should not be passed by without a quick look.

Wood End, Long Point, and the dike (map page 126), located at the west end of Provincetown Harbor, make up a typical barrier beach with salt marsh and mudflats on the inside and scrubby thickets in the dune hollows. The tidal flats attract a small number of shore-birds in season, and the thickets may have a few migrant land birds in the fall. During the late summer, flocks of terns roost on the flats at low tide and may include some Roseate Terns. Summering Black-legged Kittiwakes, invariably immatures, occasionally have appeared here in June and July, as have immature Arctic Terns. A few pelagics are sometimes seen off the beach in summer and fall.

You can park at the west-end rotary (in summer get there early) and walk out the dike to Wood End. This should be done cautiously and only at low tide, which is when the birding is best. Be very aware of the tide because the higher tides can cover the dike.

Provincetown Harbor (map page 126) is one of the best-known and most frequently birded locations in town, and is the point of departure for several whale-watching boats. It is primarily of interest in winter when it attracts Great Cormorants, a variety of sea ducks, and gulls. Iceland Gull, Glaucous Gull, Black-legged Kittiwake, and alcids are possible, the latter particularly after storms. You can check the harbor from several van-tage points, all accessible from Commercial Street (which is one way, east to west). The best of these is MacMillan Wharf, which extends well out into the harbor and offers the opportunity for excellent views of many of the birds. Alcids, when they are present (infrequently), are often very close to the wharf, even underneath it, so be sure to look over the edge. Photographers will find this to be an exceptional place to photograph several species of birds that normally can be approached only from a boat. During the winter, you can drive to the end of the wharf, but pay attention to the "No Parking" signs. In other seasons, you must park in the lot at the base of the pier (fee) and walk out the pier. During the tourist season, this area is extremely congested (and not very birdy). Public restrooms are available off the parking lot.

A couple of other public parking lots located off Commercial Street provide good views of the harbor. The best is toward the west end of town (see map page 126), just west of West Vine Street. From here an assortment of wintering waterfowl, gulls, and migrating shorebirds often can be seen. Extensive mudflats are located along the east end of the harbor at low tide, but they generally attract only a few birds.

Although some of the more productive birding spots in Provincetown are outlined above, keep in mind that the dunes throughout town are full of wet, swampy thickets and any of them might have a few birds. Keep an eye out for avian activity as you drive around the area and be prepared to do a little exploring of your own. Be aware that parking is prohibited along Race Point Road, Province Lands Road, and sections of Route 6. This ban is strictly enforced and with good reason because the sand is very soft in many areas; stick to the designated parking areas.

One means of transportation you may wish to consider is a bicycle. There is an excellent, though very hilly, bicycle trail that covers much of the town, and many of the areas outlined above are readily accessible by bike.

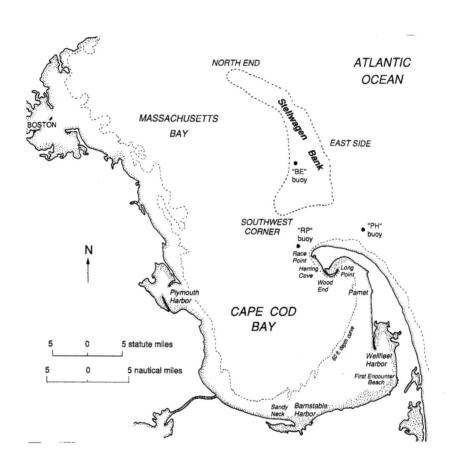

ATLANTIC
OCEAN

NORTH END

MASSACHUSETTS
BAY

BOSTON

Stellwagen Bank

EAST SIDE

"BE"
buoy

SOUTHWEST
CORNER

"PH"
buoy

"RP"
buoy

Race
Point

Herring
Cove

Long
Point

Wood
End

Pamet

N

Plymouth
Harbor

CAPE COD
BAY

60 ft. depth curve

Wellfleet
Harbor

First Encounter
Beach

5   0   5 statute miles

5   0   5 nautical miles

Sandy
Neck

Barnstable
Harbor

4

Pelagic Birding

With the proliferation of whale-watching boats, the visiting birder has ample opportunity to head seaward to observe pelagic birds. Though trips aboard tour boats, ferries, and fishing party boats are available, few travel very far offshore or can compare to the whale-watching tours that are offered from mid-April to the end of October. Provincetown is the port of departure for the majority of these boats, but trips also leave from Barnstable Harbor. Most of these trips last three to four hours. Phone numbers for the various whale-watching outfits are listed in the local yellow pages of the phone book, and all have web sites as well. When boarding a whale-watching boat, it's always a good idea to let the naturalists aboard know you're interested in birds, since that may prompt them to pay more attention to the avifauna than they normally would.

Although Cape Cod Bay can offer good seabirding during the spring and fall, in summer the pelagics are usually farther offshore. Stellwagen Bank north of Provincetown usually hosts the largest number and greatest variety of birds and is the most desirable destination for birders. Check with the whale-watching boats to find out where the whales are. Feeding concentrations of whales frequently attract large numbers of birds, though the association of seabirds and whales is by no means an absolute.

The number and species of pelagic birds in Cape Cod waters are highly variable from month to month (and even from week to week at times), but some general trends hold true.

April can be an interesting month with a diversity of sightings, but the weather is often rough offshore and the whale-watching boats (that usually start operation in mid-April) often remain in Cape Cod Bay looking for northern right whales, which are a particular specialty in early spring. Though pelagic species are generally scarce inshore during this season, a few alcids (particularly Razorbills), Red-throated and Common loons, and sea ducks such as Black, White-winged, and Surf scoters, Common Eiders, and Long-tailed Ducks are likely. Northern Gannets can be abundant in the bay at this time, as well as farther offshore, where a few Northern Fulmars may be present.

May is a transitional month. A few of the wintering Iceland Gulls and alcids may linger until midmonth. Meanwhile, migrants heading to more northerly breeding sites, such as Leach's Storm-Petrels, Red-necked Phalaropes, and jaegers pass through in small numbers. Parasitic Jaegers can sometimes be seen inshore, particularly off Herring Cove and Race Point in Provincetown, where terns and small gulls are feeding. Offshore, Wilson's Storm-Petrels and Greater and Sooty shearwaters arrive by midmonth.

From late June to mid-July, most northern hemisphere nesters are absent from Cape Cod waters, though a few nonbreeding immatures are always possible. There can be spectacular concentrations of southern hemisphere nesters—visiting during what is their nonbreeding season—in particular, Wilson's Storm-Petrels and Greater and Sooty shearwaters. This is also a good time to see Cory's Shearwaters, in years when they appear this far north, and Manx Shearwaters can be fairly common by the end of July.

Subtle changes start to occur in the marine environment during August as weak cold fronts begin pushing south. The first of the southbound migrants arrive with these fronts, while the populations of most southern-hemisphere nesters begin to decline. Greater Shearwaters remain common and are often the most plentiful species offshore. Gannets, Red-necked Phalaropes, jaegers, and even a few Sabine's Gulls arrive at this time. Parasitic Jaegers can be seen along the coast, especially where terns are feeding, while the scarcer Pomarine Jaegers are usually found only well offshore unless blown in by easterly gales. Manx Shearwaters, Red-necked Phalaropes, and Sabine's Gulls are seen most regularly over Stellwagen Bank; look for the gulls among the flocks of feeding terns. These tern flocks can comprise thousands of birds, most of which are Common Terns, though usually a few Roseate Terns are mixed in.

As the weather continues to cool in September, Northern Fulmars and a few Red Phalaropes may appear offshore. October brings a real shift in the weather as northerly winds occur with increasing regularity. Sea ducks arrive from the north in numbers, and the last of the remaining terns and most shearwaters depart to points south. Any storm-petrels seen at this time are usually Leach's, since most of the Wilson's leave by mid-September. Increasing numbers of gannets and kittiwakes arrive, the first Iceland and Glaucous Gulls appear, and Bonaparte's Gulls can be seen along the coast and in the harbors. Jaegers continue to pass through, with an increasing percentage of Pomarine Jaegers as the season wanes.

With November come the alcids. Dovekies, if they appear at all, are most likely at this time, as is the infrequently seen Atlantic Puffin. By the end of the month, Razorbills can be fairly common, and a few murres and guillemots may appear. Gannets and kittiwakes become abundant, sometimes concentrating in spectacular aggregations, both in Cape Cod Bay and offshore. A handful of Greater and Manx shearwaters and Red Phalaropes may linger until midmonth, and the last of the jaegers pass through by mid-December. By midwinter, only kittiwakes and Razorbills are likely to be present in large numbers. A few gannets typically linger through the winter, and a few guillemots may be found near shore in Provincetown. See the Cape Cod Specialties chapter (page 143) for more details on the distribution and abundance of the individual species.

Although no sea trips are regularly scheduled from Cape Cod ports after late October, occasionally trips are run out of Boston or Plymouth during the late fall and early winter; contact the Mass Audubon or the Brookline Bird Club (both have web sites) for possible trips during that time. Both organizations also occasionally offer all-day sea trips during the warmer months. These longer trips concentrate on finding birds, unlike the shorter, commercial, whale-watching trips, which are geared exclusively to finding and watching whales. Although birds are often found around the whales, this is not always the case. Watching a large concentration of birds on the distant horizon, while the boat sits dead in the water for seemingly endless periods waiting for a whale to resurface, can be an extremely frustrating experience for a birder. However, only the most jaded birders will fail to find the whales as enjoyable as the birds!

The weather at sea often differs strikingly from that on land. Temperatures, particularly in the spring and early summer, can be as much as 15 to 20 degrees colder on the water, and the wind can be appreciably stronger. Dress very warmly, regardless of the season or the weather on land, and wear a waterproof outer layer. If you are prone to seasickness, take medication before leaving land. All of the commercial whale-watching boats have heated cabins equipped with snack bars.

Those who turn green at the mere thought of stepping onto a boat need not despair of seeing pelagics. Cape Cod, extending 30 miles into the Atlantic as it does, probably offers the best chance anywhere in eastern North America of observing seabirds from land. Because of its location, Provincetown is the most consistently productive area. In almost any season or under any weather conditions, there is a possibility of seeing a few pelagics around the Race Point area, though there are many times when the sea appears devoid of avian life. The eastern shore of Chatham, particularly South Beach, is also consistently productive for land-based observations of storm-petrels, shearwaters, and jaegers. During the fall and winter, northeasterly storms may blow large numbers of pelagics into Cape Cod Bay. Several sites, notably Sandy Neck in Barnstable, Corporation Beach in Dennis, First Encounter Beach in Eastham, and Race Point in Provincetown, are vantage points from which to see these birds during, or immediately following, a storm. Refer to the appropriate sections in the preceding chapters for more information about these sites. Be aware that land-based seabirders must often endure extremely adverse weather conditions and be content with distant, and often unsatisfactory, views of their quarry. However, the spectacle of hundreds or thousands of shearwaters, storm-petrels, gannets, sea ducks, kittiwakes, and others streaming past over a churning sea is reward enough, regardless of how many individual birds go unidentified.

Least Sandpipers

5

Cape Cod Specialties

This annotated list briefly describes when and where to see a variety of species that visiting birders are typically most interested in finding. Some are essentially southern species that are near the northern edge of their range here on the Cape and are thus of greatest interest to birders visiting from the north while others are northern species near the southern edge of their range. Also included are a number of seabirds that, although generally erratic and unpredictable in their occurrence, are often more readily found in the waters around Cape Cod than anywhere else on the East Coast. The list is by no means all-inclusive, but provides a sample of the most sought-after birds.

Red-throated Loon. A common to abundant fall migrant, common winter resident and spring migrant; easy to find in November and early December along most of the Cape Cod Bay shore; Wellfleet Harbor will often provide good, close looks of the species during this season. They also are usually easy to find on the ocean-side beaches such as Nauset Beach in Orleans; usually scarce in Nantucket Sound.

Red-necked Grebe. A rather scarce, local, and inconspicuous migrant and winter resident. The best location on the Cape to see Red-necked Grebes is Corporation Beach in Dennis. A few birds are usually present here from late fall through late winter with numbers increasing, sometimes dramatically, during the early spring, when counts have occasionally exceeded 100 birds. Elsewhere, single birds are infrequently seen along the Cape Cod Bay and ocean shores, with Nauset Beach in Orleans and Race Point in Provincetown being among the most likely locales to find the species.

Northern Fulmar. A common winter resident well offshore. Only rarely seen from land, and then almost exclusively during strong northeasterly blows. Fulmars are seen sporadically on boat trips to Stellwagen Bank in the fall and early spring but are very unpredictable there.

Cory's Shearwater. An irregular summer and fall visitor. Although often the most common shearwater in the warm waters south of the Cape, the number of Cory's in Cape waters varies greatly, from essentially absent in some years to fairly common in others. When present, they often occur close to shore and can be seen from land with some regularity.

Greater Shearwater. "The" shearwater in Cape waters, the Greater is generally common to abundant from June into November and can be expected on most boat trips, and from land during storms (and occasionally at other times) at locations such as Sandy Neck, First Encounter Beach, and Provincetown.

Sooty Shearwater. A fairly common summer and uncommon fall visitor, the Sooty is the first shearwater to arrive in late May and early June, at which time it often occurs close to shore particularly in Chatham and Provincetown, and in Cape Cod Bay. The species becomes scarce by late summer, but a few usually can be found among concentrations of shearwaters through October.

Manx Shearwater. An uncommon summer and fall visitor, most often seen on Stellwagen Bank, where in some years scores may be present, or during storms from Sandy Neck or Provincetown.

Leach's Storm-Petrel. The Leach's is a rather rarely seen bird in this area despite the proximity of large nesting colonies along the coast of Maine. The species is highly pelagic, found primarily along the continental shelf far offshore, and during the nesting season is very nocturnal. In the Cape area, Leach's are most often seen from bay-side beaches such as Sandy Neck during strong northeasterly winds from August to early November. They seldom are seen on one-day boat trips, and then more often in Cape Cod Bay than on Stellwagen Bank.

Wilson's Storm-Petrel. The "default" storm-petrel in Cape waters, the Wilson's is common to abundant from late May through early September and is seen on virtually all boat trips in this season. The species also can be seen with some regularity from land at locations such as Provincetown, Chatham, and Sandy Neck, particularly during or immediately after periods of fog or onshore winds.

Northern Gannet. One of the true avian spectacles on Cape Cod is the migration of gannets along the coast. The first southbound birds appear in late August, and, by late October, they are widespread, conspicuous, and hard to miss along Cape Cod Bay and ocean beaches. Storms during this season can generate spectacular flights numbering into the many thousands of birds. Gannets generally become rather scarce by mid-January then increase again in March with the peak of the north-bound migration in April. This is an easy species to find during peak seasons, except along Nantucket Sound where it is normally scarce.

Great Cormorant. A fairly common winter resident, the Great Cormorant occurs in the largest numbers along the rocky Cape Cod Canal and Buzzards Bay shores, the ocean-side beaches of Chatham, around Nauset Inlet and Marsh, and in Provincetown. Formerly, identifying cormorants in this area involved little more than a glance at the calendar: the Double-crested was the warm-weather species and the Great was the cold-weather species. However, both species have increased and extended their seasons of occurrence so that either are possible at almost any time of the year, although the majority from late November through March are Greats and during the remainder of the year are Double-cresteds.

Brant. A common migrant and winter resident. The largest concentrations of Brant are found during the late fall feeding on the flats along the Cape Cod Bay shore from Brewster to Eastham. They also occur in numbers at Wellfleet Harbor, Nauset Marsh, Pleasant Bay, Barnstable Harbor, North Monomoy, and various beaches along Nantucket Sound.

Eurasian Wigeon. A very rare but regular migrant and winter visitor. One or two birds are often found during the fall on the ponds of South Monomoy, and wintering birds have been fairly regular, especially in Barnstable and from Chatham north to Eastham.

Barrow's Goldeneye. A rare but regular winter resident, generally found among the larger concentrations of Common Goldeneyes. The most likely sites are the south and west shores of Falmouth, Cotuit, Sandy Neck in Barnstable, Bass River in Dennis/Yarmouth, Pleasant Bay in Chatham/Orleans, and Town Cove in Orleans.

Harlequin Duck. A rare but increasingly regular winter resident; much less common here than along the rocky coasts to the north and south of the area. The only reliable site is Nauset Beach in Orleans (north of the parking lot) where several or more birds typically are present. They have also been somewhat regular at the east end of the Cape Cod Canal in Sandwich, and one or two birds occasionally show up elsewhere, especially during the late fall.

Common Eider. A common to abundant and widespread winter resident, easily found from October through May. Cape Cod lies at the heart of the wintering range for this species, with the shoals off South Monomoy often harboring thousands of individuals. In most years large flocks can be found in Sandwich near the Cape Cod Canal, at Corporation Beach in Dennis, in Provincetown, around Nauset Inlet and Nauset Beach in Orleans, in Chatham, and along the rocky shores of Woods Hole; smaller groups can be found almost anywhere along the coast. A few summering birds are often present at these sites, and the species is now breeding at a few sites in Buzzards Bay.

King Eider. A rare and irregular winter visitor, as likely to associate with flocks of scoters as with Common Eiders. This species is not easy to find and is absent some years, but check near the Cape Cod Canal in Sandwich, at Corporation Beach in Dennis, in Provincetown, and around the rocks north of the Nauset Beach parking lot in Orleans. This species is much more regular on the rocky coast north of Boston.

Black Scoter, Surf Scoter, and **White-winged Scoter.** All three species of scoters are common to abundant fall migrants with thousands, mostly Surfs and Blacks, passing along Cape Cod Bay shores from mid-September to mid-November. White-wingeds, on the other hand, are more common along ocean-side beaches. During the winter, White-wingeds are generally the most common and widespread, but small numbers of the other two species can usually be found. During this season, look for them at the mouth of the Cape Cod Canal in Sandwich, along the Buzzards Bay shoreline in Falmouth, at Corporation Beach in Dennis, at Herring Cove in Provincetown, at Nauset Beach in Orleans, and along the Nantucket Sound shoreline in Chatham and Hyannis.

Rough-legged Hawk. An irregular and increasingly rare winter visitor, this hawk is most likely in the Provincetown-Truro area, on North Beach in Orleans, at the Marstons Mills Airport, and around the Sandy Neck marshes in Barnstable. This hawk was formerly much more common, though it is still found regularly on the mainland of Massachusetts.

Bald Eagle. A rare but regular visitor in any season; seen most frequently on the outer Cape during the late spring and summer. Most are immature birds and wander widely.

Peregrine Falcon. A fairly common migrant, particularly in the fall, and a rare but regular winter resident. This magnificent bird is encountered most frequently along the immediate coast, particularly in areas where shorebirds and waterfowl congregate. The Monomoy-South Beach area of Chatham and Coast Guard Beach in Eastham are especially favored and may host several birds during the peak of migration in October. North Beach in Orleans, Sandy Neck in Barnstable, and Provincetown are also locations of regular sightings.

Northern Bobwhite. An uncommon and rapidly decreasing year-round resident. The cheerful whistle of the Bobwhite, once a regular feature of Cape Cod springs, is now heard infrequently and primarily in the more secluded brushy areas. Bobwhites are easy to locate when they are calling in the spring and early summer but can be very difficult to find during the remainder of the year. The Crane Wildlife Management Area in Falmouth, the Marstons Mills airport, and the Wellfleet

Bay Wildlife Sanctuary are areas where a few of these quail can still be found. During the winter Bobwhites join (increasingly) small coveys and visit bird feeders.

American Oystercatcher. A fairly common summer resident on the more secluded barrier beaches, particularly in the Chatham area. When present, they are generally noisy, conspicuous, and hard to miss.

Piping Plover. This federally threatened species, though still much reduced in numbers, has made a heartening recovery recently, and is a fairly common nesting species in this area, with roughly half of the state's breeding population occupying sites on Cape Cod. The largest populations are found at Sandy Neck in Barnstable, in the Monomoy-South Beach area of Chatham, and the Coast Guard Beach-North Beach area in Eastham and Orleans, but most barrier beaches support at least a pair or two. Use the utmost discretion when approaching nesting sites of this species, and, when encountering birds that appear agitated, give them a wide berth!

Migrant Shorebirds. Though any estuary or tidal flat will produce a few shorebirds during migration periods from early April through early June and early July through early November, the Monomoy-South Beach area of Chatham is the shorebird capital of Cape Cod, hosting one of the most varied and numerous concentrations of these master migrants in the Northeast. The Nauset Marsh system supports comparable numbers of some species but has fewer of the larger, less common species (e.g., Godwits, Willet, Whimbrel). Other spots that are worth checking include the Sandy Neck-Barnstable Harbor area, the Wellfleet Bay Wildlife Sanctuary, Morris Island in Chatham, West Dennis Beach, and South Cape Beach in Mashpee.

Curlew Sandpiper. A very rare and irregular migrant, most often seen at Monomoy-South Beach and, much less frequently, in the Nauset area. This species typically is found only once every year or two.

Buff-breasted Sandpiper. A rare but regular fall migrant, found during a rather brief period from late August to late September. Buff-breasteds are most often seen on Monomoy, but Coast Guard Beach in Eastham is another spot worth checking. Rarely seen on mudflats with other shorebirds, Buff-breasteds prefer dry, open areas in the upper parts of salt marshes or beach heather *(Hudsonia)* moors in dune hollows. Look particularly along the wrack line at the dune-marsh interface.

Hudsonian Godwit. A regular fall migrant in the Monomoy-South Beach area where it is easily found from early July into early September, counts occasionally exceeding 100 individuals. Elsewhere the species appears sporadically and is difficult to find. Check Morris Island in Chatham at low tide or the Nauset Marsh area where one or two are occasionally seen.

Ruff. A very rare migrant, found once every year or two on average. Most show up on Monomoy, but the Nauset area and the Wellfleet Bay Wildlife Sanctuary occasionally host one. It is found most often in July.

Red-necked Phalarope. A regular migrant offshore; seen fairly regularly in small numbers on Stellwagen Bank in late May and again from late July into September. Occasionally one or two individuals will show up on mudflats among other migrant shorebirds, particularly during late summer. Phalaropes, often in flocks, also can be seen at times from land during or immediately after easterly blows.

Red Phalarope. A regular migrant far offshore, the Red Phalarope is more pelagic than the Red-necked and less frequently seen on Stellwagen Bank or from land. Your best chance of seeing one from land is during an easterly blow in the spring or late fall; otherwise they occur primarily along the continental slope beyond the range of one-day boat trips.

Parasitic Jaeger, Pomarine Jaeger, and **Long-tailed Jaeger.** Cape Cod offers the birder one of the best chances anywhere on the East Coast of seeing jaegers from land. However, numbers are quite variable from year to year, depending upon weather and, presumably, food supply. The Parasitic is by far the most likely species inshore. Pomarine Jaegers are more common offshore but can occasionally be seen from land, particularly after easterly blows. The Long-tailed Jaeger is extremely rare onshore and seldom seen even at sea. Provincetown is one of the best locations for finding jaegers, especially when there are flocks of feeding terns present. Chatham Light and South Beach in Chatham also offer good prospects for enjoying these spectacular aerial pirates. Although a few jaegers are found every spring, far greater numbers occur from late summer through late fall. During fall storms, flocks of jaegers often get blown into Cape Cod Bay and can be seen from such locations as Sandy Neck in Barnstable, Corporation Beach in Dennis, and especially First Encounter Beach in Eastham. Jaegers are notoriously difficult to identify. Also beware of immature Laughing Gulls during the late summer and fall, which look and often behave very jaegerlike.

Little Gull. A rare but regular spring and fall migrant, the Little Gull is almost always found among flocks of Bonaparte's Gulls or terns. The Monomoy-South Beach area in late spring offers one of the best chances to find this tiny larid. From the late fall to early winter, look anywhere along the Cape Cod Bay shore or in Chatham at Chatham Light and Morris Island. Little Gulls seldom linger in any one spot on the Cape and require some luck to find.

Common Black-headed Gull. A rare migrant and winter visitor, generally found in protected estuaries, often in association with flocks of Bonaparte's Gulls or Ring-billed Gulls. A pair nested, unsuccessfully, on Monomoy in 1984, the first recorded U.S. nesting; however, none have nested since. They have been seen in a number of areas from one end of the Cape to the other, most often during the spring or fall. One or two birds are occasionally present during the winter, and wintering individuals often return to the same area in consecutive years.

Iceland Gull. A regular winter visitor in small numbers from December through March. The Provincetown area, particularly Race Point, is by far the most reliable locale, with counts of several or more individuals not uncommon. Other spots where the species is seen with some regularity include the east end of the Cape Cod Canal in Sandwich and the Chatham Fish Pier, but any concentration of wintering gulls can include an Iceland or two.

Lesser Black-backed Gull. A regular fall migrant and rare but increasing winter visitor and spring migrant; a few immatures are now regular during the summer as well. Most sightings are from the outer Cape among the large concentrations of gulls at places such as Race Point in Provincetown, the Nauset area in Eastham, Chatham Light, and Monomoy-South Beach in Chatham. Look for this species among flocks of Herring Gulls, often at the periphery, and usually not among concentrations of Great Black-backed Gulls.

Glaucous Gull. A rare but regular winter visitor, found in the same areas as Iceland Gulls; the Glaucous Gull is much the rarer of the two species. Most reports are of immature birds.

Black-legged Kittiwake. An abundant fall migrant and common winter resident offshore, regularly seen from land, often in large numbers when food is abundant or after easterly blows. A few individuals are occasionally found hanging around fishing ports such as Provincetown Harbor, the Chatham Fish Pier, and the mouth of the Cape Cod Canal. Kittiwakes are usually quite rare in Nantucket Sound and Buzzards Bay. In some years, a few immatures linger into the early summer, most often in Provincetown, at Coast Guard Beach in Eastham, or Monomoy.

Sabine's Gull. A rare but regular fall migrant and a very rare spring migrant offshore. Most reports are from Stellwagen Bank where the species is typically seen in late August or September associating with flocks of feeding terns. On rare occasions an individual will show up onshore among flocks of terns or small gulls. Otherwise, land-based observations are primarily of birds seen along the Cape Cod Bay shore during or immediately after easterly gales.

Roseate Terns

Roseate Tern. An uncommon and very local breeder and a common to abundant postbreeding visitor. Large numbers of this federally endangered species nest on inaccessible islands in Buzzards Bay and can be seen during the breeding season along the Falmouth shoreline.

A few occasionally nest in Common Tern colonies else-where on the Cape, but these colonies are ephemeral and unpredictable from year to year. Large concentrations, indeed a substantial percentage of the Roseate Terns in the Northeast, begin to appear on the Cape in late July and remain into mid-September. Peak numbers are gen-erally found on Monomoy-South Beach in Chatham, in the Nauset area, and in Provincetown, but fluctuate annu-ally, presumably in response to food supplies.

Arctic Tern. Formerly a regular breeding species, the Arctic Tern now occurs only as a rare migrant and sum-mer visitor and can be very difficult to find. A few adults pass through the outer Cape during May, and in some years small numbers of nonbreeding immatures have been present from late June into early August, concen-trating in the Monomoy-South Beach area, at Coast Guard Beach in Eastham, and in Provincetown.

Least Tern. A common and widespread nester, with colonies of varying size occurring in many areas along the Cape's coastlines. Least Tern colonies tend to be rather ephemeral, but some of the more reliable tradi-tional sites include Kalmus Park in Hyannis, West Dennis Beach in Dennis, South Beach in Chatham, Nauset Beach in Orleans, Coast Guard Beach in Eastham, the Race Point area of Provincetown, Sandy Neck in Barnstable, and the Old Harbor-Scortons Creek area of Sandwich. This remarkable little bird is the only one of the Cape's four nesting tern species to have main-tained a historically stable population in the area.

Dovekie. A very irregular late fall migrant and winter vis-itor, which is much less common than in years past. Dovekies are most likely to be seen along Cape Cod Bay beaches during or immediately after easterly blows in November and December, more rarely later in the winter. They are also fairly regular at Race Point in Provincetown, and occasionally a bird or two will show up in sheltered bays or harbors such as in Provincetown Harbor or Wellfleet Harbor, or after a strong blow grounded in backyards or along roadsides.

Common Murre. A rare winter visitor, most likely to be found off Race Point in Provincetown from December through early March; occasionally individuals appear in sheltered bays or harbors, particularly Provincetown Harbor.

Thick-billed Murre. Usually a rare winter visitor, though more numerous in some years. As with all the alcids, they are most likely to be seen in Provincetown, especially at Race Point, but occasionally show up in harbors. Sightings are also possible anywhere along the Cape Cod Bay shore during easterly storms or along ocean-side beaches.

Razorbill. A common winter resident; by far the most common of the alcids in Cape Cod waters. Numbers are quite variable from year to year, but counts into the hundreds are frequent and in some winters many thousands are present. Provincetown is the best place to see Razorbills, but they are often numerous along the entire eastern shore south to Chatham; at times, in fact, they are the most common bird on the winter ocean. Good flights also can occur along the Cape Cod Bay shore during easterly gales.

Black Guillemot. Usually a rather rare and local winter visitor. By far the most reliable place to see guillemots is the Race Point area of Provincetown; although counts of over 100 birds have been made here, in most years it is rare to see more than a couple of individuals. Elsewhere one or two are sometimes seen in Cape Cod Bay during fall storms or along ocean beaches during the winter. Guillemots are much easier to find on the rocky shores north of Cape Cod.

Atlantic Puffin. A rare and irregular fall and winter visitor. Puffins, when seen, are usually found in the same places as other alcids, but they are usually the rarest of the six species in Cape Cod waters. In some years, a few Puffins are reported from Stellwagen Bank in the late fall, and a few are occasionally seen in Cape Cod Bay during easterly gales.

Snowy Owl. A rare and irregular winter visitor, not seen every year. The most likely areas to find Snowy Owls include the Provincetown dunes, North Beach in Orleans, the Monomoy-South Beach area in Chatham, and Sandy Neck in Barnstable, but any barrier beach may host one. This dramatic bird is always much easier to find from Boston northward.

Short-eared Owl. Formerly a regular breeder on the Cape, the Short-eared Owl has decreased dramatically and is now a rare migrant and winter visitor. Reasons for its extirpation as a nester are unknown; its ecological counterpart, the Northern Harrier, still breeds in small numbers in more secluded portions of the outer Cape. Winterers and migrants may appear at any barrier beach or large open area.

Northern Saw-whet Owl. A rare and local nester, and a regular migrant and winter resident in varying numbers.

Northern Saw-whet Owl

This appealing little owl nests in a few places on the Cape, often in association with Atlantic White Cedar swamps. The cedar swamp at the Marconi Site in South Wellfleet is a favored spot as is Nickerson State Park in Brewster. Migrants and winterers may occur in almost any dense stand of evergreens.

Whip-poor-will. An uncommon and declining breeder. The loud, persistent call of the Whip-poor-will, once one of the most common and characteristic summer night sounds on Cape Cod, has now vanished from most areas. The species can still be heard in the few remnants of extensive, undisturbed woodlands, such as the pine barrens within the Cape Cod National Seashore in Wellfleet and Truro and the Crane Wildlife Management Area in Falmouth.

Northern Shrike. An irregular winter visitor, varying from absent in some years to fairly common in major flight years. They can be found in a variety of open habitats and are most common on the outer Cape. Some of the more reliable spots are Provincetown, particularly around the airport and the Herring Cove area, the High Head and Pilgrim Heights area in North Truro, the Bound Brook area in Wellfleet, Fort Hill in Eastham, the Pochet area in East Orleans, and Sandy Neck in Barnstable.

Bohemian Waxwing. An increasingly regular, though still not annual, winter visitor. Once extremely rare, this handsome boreal species has been appearing more frequently over the past decade, occasionally in large flocks. However, they are very nomadic and can be frustratingly difficult to track down. By far the most reliable areas have been in the Pamet River valley, the High Head-Pilgrim Heights area, and Old County Road, all in Truro; and in the Bound Brook area of Wellfleet.

Migrant Songbirds. One of the features of birding on Cape Cod is the occurrence of waves of migrant flycatchers, vireos, warblers, sparrows, and others during the spring and fall. When conditions are right, at least historically, thousands of songbirds appear in favored areas. Sadly, however, waves of any magnitude seem to have become mostly a fond memory as habitat destruction and other factors diminish the avifauna.

In the spring, what constitutes "prime conditions" for migrants remains difficult to define with any certainty, but generally warm southwesterly winds, particularly those associated with the northward passage of a warm front up the Atlantic seaboard, generate the best movements of migrants. Under such favorable conditions it seems that most of the birds fly over the region without stopping. It is weather that interrupts these movements, such as raw, damp northeasterly winds, that produce some of the best "fallouts" of migrants in this area.

Thus, the best days for birders, though not necessarily the birds, are those days when migration has been suddenly blocked by unfavorable weather. While these conditions may be the most consistently productive,

Yellow-rumped Warbler

significant waves of migrants have been recorded under almost all conceivable weather conditions in the spring, often with no obvious rhyme or reason. Hence, the best rule is simply to get out and look every morning from mid-April through late May, otherwise you may miss the "big one!" The premier spot for observing spring migration on the Cape is without question the Beech Forest in Provincetown. Other good locations include the High Head area in North Truro, the Wellfleet Bay Wildlife Sanctuary, Pochet Island in East Orleans, and the Ryder Conservation Area in Sandwich.

During the fall, the best birding generally follows the passage of a cold front, when winds turn northwest and temperatures drop. Some of the greatest concentrations of migrants often occur when a front stalls just offshore, interrupting migration. During this season, Provincetown remains one of the better areas for migrants, including not only the Beech Forest but also the many thickets in the area, such as those around the airport. Other places worth checking are the High Head area in North Truro; the Wellfleet Bay Wildlife Sanctuary and the Marconi Site (primarily for sparrows) in South Wellfleet; Pochet Island in East Orleans; Morris Island, most of which is privately owned and off-limits to visiting birders, and South Monomoy in Chatham.

Northern Parula. A rare and local breeder, common spring migrant, and uncommon fall migrant. The only nesting parulas in the state are on Cape Cod. The population has declined, and the species is now listed as "Special Concern" on the state's endangered and threatened species list. Remnant populations persist along the Mashpee River in Mashpee, in the Hawksnest State Park in East Harwich, and perhaps in the West Harwich Conservation Area (Bells Neck), and the Punkhorn Parklands in Brewster. Migrants are found in the typical land bird traps listed above.

Pine Warbler. A very common and widespread nester, common spring migrant, uncommon fall migrant, and rare winter resident in pine barrens and mixed pine-oak woodlands. The musical trill of the Pine Warbler is one of the most frequent sounds in the Cape's woodlands, and the visiting birder should have no trouble locating this species during the spring and early summer. Pine Warblers become much more difficult to find once they stop singing in midsummer but usually can be located by diligent searching in the pine barrens for roving, mixed-species flocks of passerines, their rather loud chips often revealing their presence. A few Pine Warblers usually attempt to winter, when they often show up at suet feeders.

Prairie Warbler. A fairly common, but declining, nester in overgrown fields, scrubby pine barrens, and power line cuts; an uncommon migrant. The Prairie Warbler is widespread and fairly easy to find during the summer in areas with extensive growth of red cedar or dry, sparse stands of pitch pine. Some good sites are the Crane Wildlife Management Area in Falmouth, the Marstons Mills Airport, Fort Hill in Eastham, the Wellfleet Bay Wildlife Sanctuary, the Marconi Site in South Wellfleet, and around the Cape Cod National Seashore visitor center in Provincetown. However, development and natural succession are eliminating much of this species' preferred habitat.

Grasshopper Sparrow. A very rare and local nester, which has declined drastically over the past several decades and is now in danger of disappearing altogether as a breeder on the Cape. The only nesting sites remaining are the Crane Wildlife Management Area in Falmouth, which supports just a few pairs, and the Massachusetts Military Reservation, which is off-limits to the public.

Seaside Sparrow. A rare and very local nester and a rare fall migrant and winter visitor. The only area Seaside Sparrows are known to nest is the Great Marsh in Barnstable, where at least several pairs are usually present. The best chance for finding the species during the fall and early winter is Fort Hill in Eastham during times when abnormally high tides flood the marsh and force both Seaside and Saltmarsh Sharp-tailed sparrows out of the marsh and into the grass and shrubs at the base of the hill. Under these conditions, you may also have some luck around the edge of the marsh at First Encounter Beach in Eastham or at the end of Navigation Road in Barnstable. You will probably have to get your feet wet to see this bird!

Vesper Sparrow. A rare, local, and declining nester, and a rare fall migrant. The Vesper Sparrow, like the Grasshopper Sparrow, was once widespread across the Cape but has now all but vanished as a breeder. The only known nesting sites remaining are the Marconi Site in South Wellfleet and in some of the dunes around

Roosting Peeps

Provincetown and the High Head area in North Truro, though the species seems to be on the brink of disappearing even from these protected areas.

Lapland Longspur. An uncommon fall migrant and winter visitor, most often found among flocks of Horned Larks frequenting the short grassy areas of barrier beaches. Some of the best spots are the Race Point-Provincetown Municipal Airport area, North Beach in Orleans, Monomoy-South Beach, Crosby Landing in Brewster, Chapin Beach in Dennis, and Sandy Neck in Barnstable.

Snow Bunting. A common late fall migrant and uncommon winter resident, typically frequenting areas of extensive dunes along the outer beaches. Good locations include the dunes along the ocean side from Provincetown to North Truro, Coast Guard Beach and First Encounter Beach in Eastham, North Beach in Orleans, Monomoy-South Beach in Chatham, Hardings Beach in Chatham, West Dennis and Chapin beaches in Dennis, and Sandy Neck in Barnstable.

6

Checklist of the Birds of Cape Cod

This checklist contains 317 species that have been recorded on Cape Cod at least 10 times during the last 20 years. The taxonomic sequence follows the 7th edition of the *American Ornithologist's Union Checklist of the Birds of North America* (1998). Each species' status through the seasons is shown by means of a bar graph. The list was compiled most recently in 2002.

KEY:

▬	= Abundant and widespread; easily found and often in very large numbers.
	= Common; easily found in the proper habitat.
▬	= Uncommon and/or local; generally seen only in small numbers or within very restricted habitats.
	= Rare but regular; recorded every year but usually hard to find.
	= Very rare and irregular; not seen every year.

CODES:

∗ = Nesting confirmed during the last decade.
+ = Nesting suspected but not confirmed during the last decade.
E = Erratic; numbers highly variable from year to year.
P = Pelagic; checklist indicates status near shore, including Stellwagen Bank, rather than offshore.
↑ = Species has increased locally in recent years.
↓ = Species has decreased locally in recent years.

Report sightings of any rare species to:
Wellfleet Bay Wildlife Sanctuary, South Wellfleet (508-349-2615)
Birdwatcher's General Store, Orleans (508-255-6974)

		JAN	FEB	MAR	APR	MAY	JUN	JUL	AUG	SEP	OCT	NOV	DEC
Loon, Red-throated													
Pacific													
Common													
Grebe, Pied-billed													
Horned													
Red-necked													
Fulmar, Northern	P												
Shearwater, Cory's	P												
Greater	P												
Sooty	P												
Manx	P												
Storm-Petrel, Wilson's	P												
Leach's	P												
Gannet, Northern													
Cormorant, Double-crested	*↑												
Great													
Bittern, American													
Least	+												
Heron, Great Blue													
Egret, Great	*												
Snowy	*												
Heron, Little Blue													
Tricolored													
Egret, Cattle													
Heron, Green	*↓												
Night-Heron, Black-crowned	*												
Yellow-crowned													
Ibis, Glossy													
Vulture, Black	↑												
Turkey	+↑												
Goose, Snow	↑												
Canada	*												
Brant													
Swan, Mute	*↑												
Duck, Wood	*												
Gadwall	*												
Wigeon, Eurasian													
American	*												
Duck, American Black	*												
Mallard	*												
Teal, Blue-winged	*												
Shoveler, Northern	*												
Pintail, Northern	*												
Teal, Green-winged	*												
Canvasback	↓												
Redhead													

164

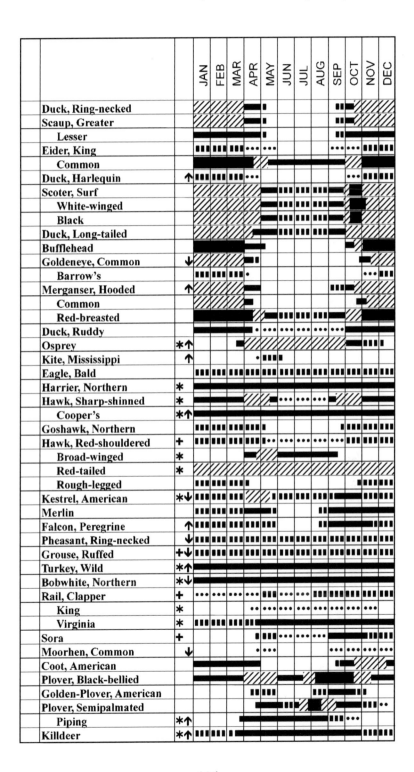

	JAN	FEB	MAR	APR	MAY	JUN	JUL	AUG	SEP	OCT	NOV	DEC
Duck, Ring-necked												
Scaup, Greater												
Lesser												
Eider, King												
Common												
Duck, Harlequin												
Scoter, Surf												
White-winged												
Black												
Duck, Long-tailed												
Bufflehead												
Goldeneye, Common												
Barrow's												
Merganser, Hooded												
Common												
Red-breasted												
Duck, Ruddy												
Osprey												
Kite, Mississippi												
Eagle, Bald												
Harrier, Northern												
Hawk, Sharp-shinned												
Cooper's												
Goshawk, Northern												
Hawk, Red-shouldered												
Broad-winged												
Red-tailed												
Rough-legged												
Kestrel, American												
Merlin												
Falcon, Peregrine												
Pheasant, Ring-necked												
Grouse, Ruffed												
Turkey, Wild												
Bobwhite, Northern												
Rail, Clapper												
King												
Virginia												
Sora												
Moorhen, Common												
Coot, American												
Plover, Black-bellied												
Golden-Plover, American												
Plover, Semipalmated												
Piping												
Killdeer												

		JAN	FEB	MAR	APR	MAY	JUN	JUL	AUG	SEP	OCT	NOV	DEC
Oystercatcher, American	*↑												
Yellowlegs, Greater													
Lesser													
Sandpiper, Solitary													
Willet	*↑												
Sandpiper, Spotted	*↓												
Upland	*↓												
Whimbrel													
Godwit, Hudsonian													
Marbled													
Turnstone, Ruddy													
Knot, Red													
Sanderling													
Sandpiper, Semipalmated													
Western													
Least													
White-rumped													
Baird's													
Pectoral													
Purple													
Dunlin													
Sandpiper, Curlew													
Stilt													
Buff-breasted													
Ruff													
Dowitcher, Short-billed													
Long-billed													
Snipe, Common													
Woodcock, American	*↓												
Phalarope, Wilson's													
Red-necked	P												
Red	P												
Skua, Great	P												
Jaeger, Pomarine	P												
Parasitic	P												
Long-tailed	P												
Gull, Laughing	*												
Little													
Black-headed													
Bonaparte's													
Ring-billed													
Herring	*↓												
Iceland													
Lesser Black-backed	↑												
Glaucous													
Great Black-backed	*↑												

166

Species	Status	JAN	FEB	MAR	APR	MAY	JUN	JUL	AUG	SEP	OCT	NOV	DEC
Gull, Sabine's	P												
Kittiwake, Black-legged	P												
Tern, Caspian													
Royal													
Sandwich													
Roseate	*												
Common	*												
Arctic	*↓												
Forster's													
Least	*												
Black													
Skimmer, Black	*												
Dovekie	P												
Murre, Common	P												
Thick-billed	P												
Razorbill													
Guillemot, Black													
Puffin, Atlantic	P												
Dove, Rock	*												
Mourning	*												
Cuckoo, Black-billed	*												
Yellow-billed	*												
Owl, Barn													
Screech-Owl, Eastern	*↑												
Owl, Great Horned	*												
Snowy													
Long-eared													
Short-eared	↓												
Northern Saw-whet	*												
Nighthawk, Common													
Chuck-will's-widow	+↑												
Whip-poor-will	*↓												
Swift, Chimney	*												
Hummingbird, Ruby-throated	*												
Kingfisher, Belted	*												
Woodpecker, Red-headed													
Red-bellied	*↑												
Sapsucker, Yellow-bellied													
Woodpecker, Downy	*												
Hairy	*												
Flicker, Northern	*												
Flycatcher, Olive-sided													
Wood-Pewee, Eastern	*												
Flycatcher, Yellow-bellied													
Acadian													
Alder													

Species	Status	JAN	FEB	MAR	APR	MAY	JUN	JUL	AUG	SEP	OCT	NOV	DEC
Willow	*												
Least													
Phoebe, Eastern	*												
Flycatcher, Great Crested	*												
Kingbird, Western													
Eastern	*												
Shrike, Northern													
Vireo, White-eyed	+												
Yellow-throated													
Blue-headed													
Warbling	*												
Philadelphia													
Red-eyed	*												
Jay, Blue	*												
Crow, American	*												
Fish	*↑												
Lark, Horned	*												
Martin, Purple													
Swallow, Tree	*												
Northern Rough-winged	*												
Bank	*												
Cliff													
Barn	*												
Chickadee, Black-capped	*												
Titmouse, Tufted	*↑												
Nuthatch, Red-breasted	*E												
White-breasted	*↑												
Creeper, Brown	*												
Wren, Carolina	*↑												
House	*												
Winter													
Marsh	*												
Kinglet, Golden-crowned	E												
Ruby-crowned													
Gnatcatcher, Blue-gray	*												
Bluebird, Eastern	*↑												
Veery													
Thrush, Gray-cheeked													
Bicknell's													
Swainson's													
Hermit	*												
Wood	*↓												
Robin, American	*												
Catbird, Gray	*												
Mockingbird, Northern	*												
Thrasher, Brown	*↓												

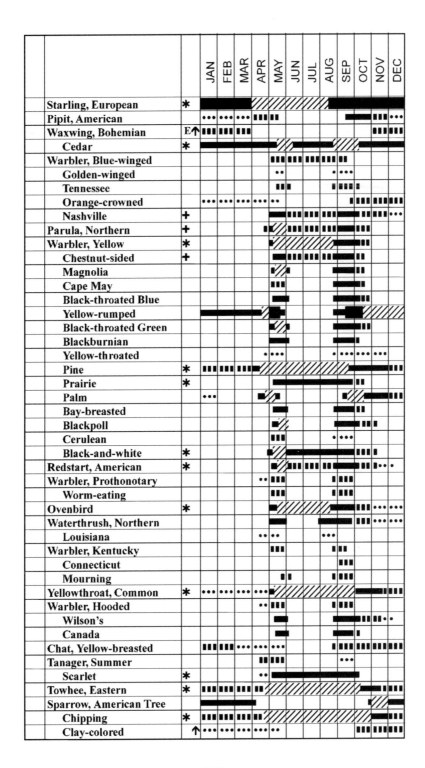

		JAN	FEB	MAR	APR	MAY	JUN	JUL	AUG	SEP	OCT	NOV	DEC
Starling, European	*												
Pipit, American													
Waxwing, Bohemian	E↑												
Cedar	*												
Warbler, Blue-winged													
Golden-winged													
Tennessee													
Orange-crowned													
Nashville	+												
Parula, Northern	+												
Warbler, Yellow	*												
Chestnut-sided	+												
Magnolia													
Cape May													
Black-throated Blue													
Yellow-rumped													
Black-throated Green													
Blackburnian													
Yellow-throated													
Pine	*												
Prairie	*												
Palm													
Bay-breasted													
Blackpoll													
Cerulean													
Black-and-white	*												
Redstart, American	*												
Warbler, Prothonotary													
Worm-eating													
Ovenbird	*												
Waterthrush, Northern													
Louisiana													
Warbler, Kentucky													
Connecticut													
Mourning													
Yellowthroat, Common	*												
Warbler, Hooded													
Wilson's													
Canada													
Chat, Yellow-breasted													
Tanager, Summer													
Scarlet	*												
Towhee, Eastern	*												
Sparrow, American Tree													
Chipping	*												
Clay-colored	↑												

169

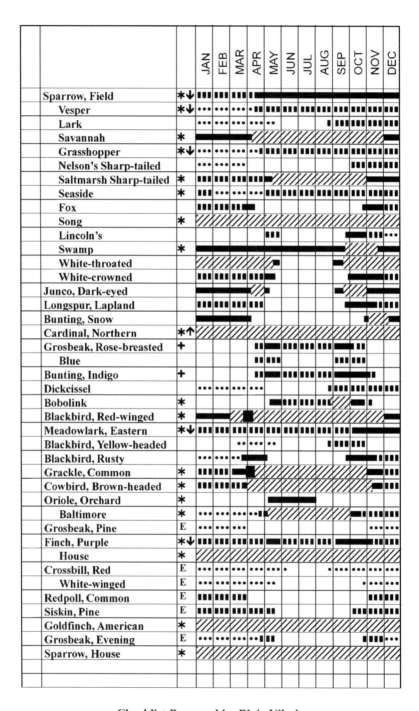

Checklist Prepared by Blair Nikula

INDEX

180

ABOUT THE AUTHORS

Mass Audubon is the largest conservation organization in New England, concentrating its efforts on protecting the nature of Massachusetts for people and wildlife. It protects more than 30,000 acres of conservation land in Massachusetts, conducts educational programs for 250,000 children and adults annually, and advocates for sound environmental policies at the local, state, and federal levels. Established in 1896, and supported by 68,000 member households, Mass Audubon maintains 42 wildlife sanctuaries that are open to the public and serve as the base for its conservation, education, and advocacy work across the state. For more information or to become a member, call 800-AUDUBON (283-8266) or visit the website at www.massaudubon.org.

The Cape Cod Bird Club was organized in 1972 and rapidly grew to become one of the largest bird clubs in the state. The club meets on the second Monday of each month, September through May, and conducts several walks per month to locations both on and off Cape Cod. Visitors are always welcome at any club activities. Additionally, the club sponsors several research projects, including a breeding bird census, winter birdfeeder and waterfowl censuses, and the Mid-Cape Christmas Bird Count. Visit us online at www.massbird.org/ccbc.

On Cape Publications, Inc. specializes in Cape Cod and New England books, including some of the region's best natural history books and guides. These include *In the Footsteps of Thoreau: 25 Historic & Nature Walks on Cape Cod, A Guide to Nature on Cape Cod & the Islands, Walking the Shores of Cape Cod, Quabbin: A History & Explorer's Guide, The Innermost Waters: Fishing Cape Cod's Ponds & Lakes* and *Cape Cod, Martha's Vineyard & Nantucket, the Geologic Story.* Look for them and other books by On Cape Publications, Inc. at your local bookstore or on the web at www.oncapepublications.com.